Twayne's United States Authors Series

SYLVIA E. BOWMAN, *Editor*

INDIANA UNIVERSITY

Timothy Dwight

TIMOTHY DWIGHT

TIMOTHY DWIGHT

by KENNETH SILVERMAN
New York University

145

Twayne Publishers, Inc. : : New York

Library of Congress Catalog Card Number: 6824303

MANUFACTURED IN THE UNITED STATES OF AMERICA

TIMOTHY DWIGHT

by

KENNETH SILVERMAN

Timothy Dwight discusses the literary career of one of the most bitterly denounced and most passionately defended public figures of eighteenth century America. Grandson of Jonathan Edwards, President of Yale, Dwight kept alive, more than anyone else in the American enlightenment, the spirit of seventeenth-century New England. During the long and intense public debate on the nature and aims of the new republic, he was the most influential spokesman for the Federalist-Congregationalist point of view.

Professor Silverman's study describes Dwight's thinking on such major issues of his time as property rights, Deism, and the French Revolution, by analyzing in detail his major works: *The Conquest of Canäan, Greenfield Hill, The Triumph of Infidelity,* and the *Travels; In New-England and New York.* But for the most part it charts the evolution of Dwight's feelings about America. An ardent sponsor of Independence and national unity in his youth, he ended his life as the celebrant of Connecticut, in an America he felt would always be alien to him and to his class. In between, his feelings constantly changed in response to the political, social, and religious crises of his era.

(Continued from front flap)

Influential as a social theorist, as an educator, and as a theologian, Dwight was also outstanding among the group of poets known as the Connecticut Wits. As a poet and essayist he was deeply concerned with the problem of creating an American literature that would express the emerging American personality. By showing how for Dwight the literary problem of creating an American literature was inseparable from the social and political problems of creating America itself, this book tries to provide an approach to early American literature as a whole.

Preface

THE MIND of Timothy Dwight, said Vernon Louis Parrington, "was closed as tight as his study windows in January." "Stuffy" is the traditional verdict on Timothy Dwight, the Pope of Federalism, the echo of the past. Yet with the greatest enthusiasm he shared the thinking and the tone of his most farsighted contemporaries. He shared Tom Paine's hope that in his time mankind would renew itself, and Thomas Jefferson's that the model for mankind's renewal would be America. His career spanned the American Enlightenment, and his verse and prose spoke for its aspirations.

But Parrington was right. No other man in Dwight's time hated Paine or Jefferson more. The same Dwight who hoped for the rebirth of humanity foresaw its apocalyptic death: "It is the day of the Lord's vengeance; the year of recompenses for the Controversies of Zion. The Earth is utterly broken down, the earth is clean dissolved; the earth is moved exceedingly." The same Dwight who believed that America would generate the renewal of man saw America "converted into one theatre of falsehood, perjury, fraud, theft, piracy, robbery, oppression, revenge, fornication and adultery."

In this sense Timothy Dwight was a manichean. Through his belief in progress and his chiliasm, through Washington and Jefferson, Federalists and Republicans, Calvin and Voltaire, America and Europe, he perceived the eternal warfare between good and evil. He lived only on birthday or doomsday. He rarely felt less than completely horrified or completely joyful. His gross reverses of feeling, however, cannot be explained merely by his having entertained varying theories of history. They resulted from real upheavals in his time, which caused him real shocks. His doomsday rhetoric of broken cisterns, or his birthday rhetoric of rising empires, always addressed political and social realities. To fully understand his writings one must translate the broken cisterns into Jefferson or Shays, the rising empires into Washington or Eli Whitney. To do so, would be to write a history of New England between the Revolution and the War of 1812. This brief study attempts nothing so elaborate. It mentions the history of Dwight's time only to explain the alterations of his rhetoric and, consequently, to explain his impatience with the American experiment.

During these alterations, these total hopes and total despairs, Dwight kept unchanged a single modest conviction. It is epitomized by a dictum of William Penn's which Dwight quoted in one of his last essays:

> Nothing is necessary to make good men harmonious and friendly but that they should live near to each other, and converse often, kindly, and freely, with each other.

Dwight believed this more than he believed anything else. On whatever issue he engaged his contemporaries, it was for the sake of validating this one proposition. In his own life its truth was confirmed by the peacefulness and happiness of the Connecticut Valley. He regarded the family-style institutions which produced that peace and happiness as the inevitable bases of American society.

While discussing Dwight's views on American society and tracing his disenchantment with America, I have tried at all times to maintain contact with Dwight the literary man. He was one of the first American poets who hoped to disburden himself of English poetry. In his epic poem, *The Conquest of Canäan,* he tried to accommodate English verse conventions to his intensely local materials. Later, in his long pastoral poem, *Greenfield Hill,* he tried very hesitantly to invent a native literary idiom. In both cases he failed; and, before he was forty, he stopped trying (the latter half of this study deals nearly exclusively with his prose). The crude originality of his verse reveals the trials of colonial literary life, the difficulties of writing in a borrowed culture. Even his literary career, then, leads one back to his thinking about America. The nature and quality of his verse express his hope that a Connecticut-style America would challenge and overcome Europe in artistic achievement. He gave up writing verse because of his impatience with America itself. For him, as for almost every other writer of his place and time, the great fact of the imagination was America; literature was history, history was literature.

KENNETH SILVERMAN

Once again my thanks go to Professor Lewis Leary, this time for turning over to me his office in the Columbia University Library, and allowing me to browse at will in his magnificent files of early American literature.

K. S.

Contents

Chronology

1752 Timothy Dwight born May 14 in Northampton, Massachusetts; his father, a merchant; his mother, the third daughter of Jonathan Edwards. Under her tutelage he read the Bible easily at the age of four; shortly after tried teaching the catechism to Indians.

1765 Admitted to Yale but distracted from his studies by a broken arm, unsettled conditions after the Stamp Act, and a fleeting addiction to gambling. Soon began studying fourteen hours a day.

1771 Appointed tutor at Yale, along with John Trumbull. Lectured on style and composition. Wrote a "Song," "America," "The Trial of Faith," "Esther and Mordecai," and began composing *The Conquest of Canäan.*

1772 Awarded M.A. Delivered at the public commencement "A Dissertation on the History, Eloquence, and Poetry of the Bible."

1774 Entered the college church. In the summer, his eyes ruined by study; suffered increasingly violent attacks of colic; returned to Northampton.

1777 March: married Mary Woolsey. June: licensed as preacher and began preaching at Weathersfield. Continued teaching his Yale classes there, where they had removed from the battle lines. August: completed a draft of *The Conquest of Canäan.* September: appointed chaplain to Parson's brigade; joined the army at West Point in October.

1778 March: wrote to Washington from camp, asking permission to dedicate the *Conquest* to him. October: news of his father's death reached him from Natchez. Returned to

Northampton to support his mother and twelve siblings for the next five years.

1783 November: ordained pastor of the Congregational church at Greenfield, where he stayed twelve years. Established a coeducational academy which attracted students from all over the Union and from Yale.

1785 Published *The Conquest of Canäan.* Wrote "Epistle . . . to Col. Humphreys" and "The Critics."

1787 Received Doctor of Divinity degree from Princeton.

1788 *The Triumph of Infidelity* published, anonymously. July: Noah Webster defended the *Conquest* against British reviewers in the *American Magazine* for July 4. In the same issue Webster adversely criticized the *Triumph,* apparently unaware of Dwight's authorship.

1794 *Greenfield Hill* published.

1795 May: Ezra Stiles died. September: Dwight inaugurated as president of Yale. Openly argued with campus infidels on the authenticity of Scripture, and soon reversed the tide of Infidelism. In the course of his reign he tripled Yale's enrollment, instituted a new system of discipline, and as Professor of Divinity wrote *Theology.*

1796 Began horseback journeys during college vacations for exercise; meanwhile, collected material for his *Travels.*

1797 Asked by the General Association of Connecticut to revise Barlow's edition of Watts's *Psalms.* September: preached two discourses on "The Nature, and Danger, of Infidel Philosophy."

1798 May: Jedediah Morse announced the existence of an Illuminist conspiracy to overturn religion and liberty in America. July 4: Dwight preached "The Duty of Americans, at the Present Crisis," amidst rising war fever. His outspokenness prompted public attacks against "Pope Dwight" and against Yale.

1801 February: election of Jefferson. To fight the new administration Dwight founded the Federalist *Palladium,* and began contributing to it voluminously and anonymously.

1802 Great religious revival at Yale. For the next ten years, much heartened, he wrote extensively and exclusively on social and missionary topics.

1812 Attacked the war in "A Discourse . . . on the Public Fast."

1815 Defended American culture while pleading for a special Anglo-Yankee partnership in *Remarks on the Review of Inchiquin's Letters.*

1816 "Observations on the Present State of Religion in the World."

1817 Oliver Wolcott elected by a Republican-Episcopalian majority, ending the Federalist regime in Connecticut. January 11: Dwight died. Business in New Haven suspended for his funeral. Sermons and public services throughout the country marked his death.

1818 *Theology.* New written Constitution for Connecticut, supplanting the Charter of 1662.

1821 *Travels; In New-England and New York.*

Timothy Dwight

CHAPTER *1*

The Ideal America

I *Tutorship*

MR. DWIGHT," wrote John Trumbull of his fellow tutor at Yale, "is to be our American poet."[1] Given the atmosphere at Yale in 1770, it was an improbable destiny. Morale was low; the curriculum, thin; the teaching, so the students regularly complained, insipid. And outside Yale was drift, the restlessness of the period between the French and the Revolutionary wars. Toward becoming "our American poet," Dwight could contribute, at nineteen, a taste for verse; a fervent nationalism; a tolerance for self-discipline; and, not least, a driving ambitiousness.

Genius Dwight would later define as a large capacity for exertion. During his third year as tutor, to check dullness of mind, he subsisted on twelve mouthfuls of vegetables each meal. He punished eyes already weakened by a smallpox inoculation with parsing a hundred lines of Homer by candlelight each dawn, followed by fourteen hours of study. His regime, severe and paradoxical, was that of Dwight the champion of Enlightenment, who hailed the vaccine as a sign of inevitable progress, and who wrote in eleven books of couplets the first American epic; but its rabbinical austerity belonged to Dwight the grandson of Jonathan Edwards, to one of the last great New England Calvinist ministers. And its severity brought on twenty violent attacks of bilious colic, interrupting Dwight's career and causing a worried father to fetch back to the family home at Northampton his emaciated and nearly blind son.

Yale in 1770 might nourish the Puritan cleric in Dwight, but not the disciple of progress, not "our American poet." Dwight vigorously and deeply shared the conservative values which Yale hoped to give Connecticut youth, and later he became their shrillest spokesman. But he deplored the absence of literary studies in the curriculum. Such studies, under William Smith at the College of Philadelphia, had nurtured Nathaniel Evans, Francis Hopkinson, and Thomas Godfrey, a whole generation of native poets. Although some quasi-literary societies had been organized at Yale in the 1760's, while Dwight was an undergraduate, they were designed to train students for law and public office by allowing them to compose and deliver speeches. During their tutorships, Dwight and Trumbull transformed these societies into courses in English composition.

Dwight lectured informally on style after school hours, encouraged the writing and declamation of his students, and offered a prize book for the best essay. As a result, despite the prevailing student unrest, and although many students were older than he, Dwight became an immensely popular teacher. President Ezra Stiles, who felt his own authority threatened by Dwight's appeal, believed Dwight encouraged student revolts against the administration. Indeed, the senior class twice petitioned the Yale corporation to hire Dwight to teach them rhetoric and belles lettres, in addition to his assigned duties. Very reluctantly, the corporation granted the petition; but, as a gesture of its continued control over the curriculum, it required interested students to have their parents' consent. Under Dwight and Trumbull the existent instruction in public speaking resulted in a vogue for studying and writing non-political literature. At Yale, Benjamin Silliman recalled, Dwight "overthrew the dominion of false taste, both in composition and elocution," and established "a standard both of poetry and prose, pure, classical and dignified. . . ."[2]

During his tutorship Dwight's own literary career began. Most of his apprentice works are self-conscious displays of taste, exercises in correctness. Yet they touch on themes that occupied him all of his life. He may have assisted Trumbull in writing some *Spectator*-like essays, "The Meddler" and "The Correspondent," a form to which he returned in his later nationalistic essays, "The Friend." He wrote two biblical poems: "Esther and Mordecai" and "The Trial of Faith" (the story of Daniel) in which he followed the practice of Cowley and Pope, among others (and of a colonial Connecticut poet, Roger Wolcott, whose poems were in the Yale library), of expanding Scripture into heroic couplets and a sublime style. Both poems prepared Dwight for his biblical epic, *The Conquest of Canäan,* and for that application of biblical prophecy to the present which guides his later jeremiads against Jefferson and France. His interest in music led him to collect sacred songs and to write a "Song" ("Look, lovely maid, on yonder flow'r"), modeled on Herrick, an interest he later elaborated in his edition of Watts's *Psalms*. Disapproving his own ambitiousness, and sensitive to criticism, he delayed publishing these poems for another fifteen years.

The apprentice poem most akin to Dwight's mature verse is "America: Or, a Poem on the Settlement of the British Colonies." Trumbull, who read the poem in 1771 when it circulated in manuscript at Yale, wrote that Dwight intended "only a general view of America by way of tryal of his genius."[3] Ezra Stiles, however, assumed Dwight wrote it "so to commend him to the Army, the Assemblies & Congress that it would make his fortune, by Procurg him some office. . . ."[4] Always leery of Dwight, Stiles neglected to say that he had published the poem ten years after writing it, and then anonymously. Stiles's distrust reflects the fact that for many writers of the early republic, such as Joel Barlow, David Humphreys, and Philip Freneau, literature provided, like law on a larger scale, an entry into public life, a relationship which Dwight's courses in belles lettres were designed to end. Trumbull was right: in three hundred lines of heroic couplets, Dwight was testing his voice, expressing hopes for America that Yale undergraduates expected themselves to have, in the elevated tone they thought they should feel.

One might have heard the same ideals, in nearly the same language, professed in Pennsylvania, in New York, or in New Jersey. At Princeton, the year Dwight wrote "America," Philip Freneau and Hugh Henry Brackenridge devoted unbounded hyperbole to their similar sense of America's vastness, its opportunities for the oppressed, its friendliness to genius.[5] Trumbull himself had written comparable verses on America's destiny for the Yale commencement a year earlier. In practice, however, these nationalistic ideals often outraged Dwight's religious beliefs. From that strain results the novelty of his career. He spent his life now boosting those ideals, now blasting them: one moment he was a Babbitt; the next, Jeremiah.

The first half of "America" recounts the colonial past through Columbus, the Puritans, William Penn, James Oglethorpe, and the French wars; the remainder prophesies the future, crowned by a brief vision of the millennium. Like other contemporary treatments of America's destiny, Dwight's Virgilian, prophetic pose and his tone of public patriotic address echo Pope's "Messiah" and "Windsor Forest," published more than half a century earlier. "America" thus expresses a continued cultural lag in the colonies. When Pope began writing, that is when the language of "America" was still fresh, Edward Taylor was still imitating George Herbert. Accordingly, it is not the observed potential of Dwight's present place and time that informs his vision of the future, but Pope's mythicized revival of the Roman Augustan age.

The America Dwight predicts in 1771—the imperial giant, the epitome of the best of the past, resplendent with royal architecture, exotic perfumes, "temples starr'd with gems and roof'd with gold"—is largely the ideal England of 1712. In 1712 Pope saw England in "Messiah" as expanding into sprawling cities, swarming with life: "See, a long race thy spacious courts adorn,/See future sons, and daughters yet unborn,/In crowding ranks on every side arise,/Demanding life, impatient for the skies!" In 1771, a half-century later, Dwight applied Pope's vision to America, and foresaw a teeming continent: "See num'rous infant states begin to grow;/See every state with peace and plenty flow;/See splendid towns o'er all the land extend";[6] and "Round thy broad fields more glorious ROMES arise,/With pomp and splendour bright'ning all the skies."

The catalogues, the diction, the tone of exclamatory surprise, are all Pope's, particularly the rhyming of "rise" and "skies"—a rhyming pair Dwight used in later verse ad nauseam. It suited perfectly his manichean temperament, his willingness to see the world as sunken or soaring, white or black, in a perpetual state of "Triumph" or "Conquest." Dwight did work some changes on Pope's language. Where Pope, describing American commerce, foresees "the new world launch forth to seek the old," Dwight sees "the *old* world rejoic'd to see the *new*." His syntax and italics playfully emphasize a new relation between England and her colonies by granting America ascendant interest. And, while "America" extolls English heroism in the French and Indian wars, it also criticizes the England of Laud where "BRITONS were learn'd to torture, laws t'obey." For Dwight was not merely reworking outworn English conventions; he was defending betrayed English values. America's great task, Dwight and other colonists believed, was to preserve, in defiance of the very England that had forsaken them, such hallowed English values as liberty.

The two poems differ most, however, in the bases for their nationalistic hopes. Pope predicts a glorious future on the evidence of the past. Windsor Forest brings to his mind Surrey, Denham, Cowley, a heritage of poets and kings whose very names assure promise for the future. But Dwight could not find such assurances in the America of his time. Unable to speak from Pope's richly suggestive Windsor, he places himself in a "lonesome vale," where not Surrey and Denham but an abstract "Spirit of Freedom" must forecast the triumph of Philosophy, Science, Religion, Sculpture, Poetry, and Eloquence in America.

Dwight's problem, which he shared with all other early American poets, was how to be specific but not parochial. America had no Surreys or Cowleys to speak of, and homely local subjects, Dwight soon discovered, brought puzzlement or amused condescension from English reviewers. Dwight's growth as a poet was inseparable from the consolidation of the Union. To be specific, to address his own condition, meant an increased freedom in the use of local subject matter. And this awaited a heightened *pietas,* a reverence for the communal life. Only a national audience aware of Jefferson and Shays would allow Dwight boldly to translate the "lonesome vale" into the Connecticut Valley and the "Spirit of Freedom" into the Congregational clergy.

Meanwhile, lacking a Cowley or a King Charles, Dwight has the millennium serve the function of history and makes a national hero out of God. He suddenly suspends the wholly secular imagery of the poem to insert a hymn to God the nation-builder: "At thy command, war glitters o'er the plain; /Thou speak'st—and peace revives the fields again, /Vast empires rise, and cities gild the day." This same force, Dwight implies, will create the glorious future of the yet unstoried America. America does not need a heritage of poets and kings because it has God. Similarly, Dwight uses the millennium, as Pope used the Stuarts, to justify America's imperial role. To prepare for its millennial destiny America will extend its sway across the world until "savage nations at thy scepter bend." In this way Dwight made God and the millennium fill out the thin promise of his culture. Otherwise, his youthful vision of America, like that of many a commencement poet in the colonies, was largely the creation of Pope.

II *The Growth of* The Conquest of Canäan

In 1771, while "America" circulated in manuscript at Yale, Dwight began writing his epic poem. *The Conquest of Canäan* is essentially an expansion of the central chapters of the Book of Joshua. The bulk of it recounts the Israelite battles against the peoples of Ai and Gibeon, culminating in Joshua's victory over the Canaanites. The biblical action, occupying only four short chapters, is filled out into eleven books of closed couplets by the addition of lengthy speeches, protracted battle scenes, epic devices, testimonials to American heroes, and a love story.

The poem underwent three distinct stages of revision before its publication in 1785. By 1775 Dwight had completed a first draft, and a year later had printed proposals for its publication, which the imminent Revolution made impossible. A second stage of composition began when Dwight returned to Yale as a senior tutor in 1777; presumably as a gift to his new bride, he then inserted into his completed epic two whole new books, Three and Five, comprising the romance of Irad and Selima, a fatal irrelevance. Shortly after, Congress approved Dwight as chaplain to Parson's First Connecticut Brigade, part of the army guarding the Hudson River at Peekskill. Here the poem underwent additional revision as his experiences at camp inspired Dwight to add assorted panegyrics to Revolutionary heroes.

During this stage of composition, in March, 1778, Dwight wrote to Washington at Valley Forge, asking permission to dedicate to him the yet uncompleted poem. He presented himself as "so independent a Republican, and so honest a man, as to be incapable of a wish to palm myself upon the world under the patronage of another. . . ." He explained that his endeavor was "not common in the American regions," a poem "on the *Conquest of Canaan* [*sic*], *by Joshua.*"[7] By adding "Joshua" to the title, Dwight no doubt intended hinting to Washington that he figured in the poem. Dwight later denied any relationship between his hero and Washington, and omitted "Joshua" from the published title. Washington, who had not seen the poem, replied ten days later from Valley Forge that nothing could please him more "than to patronize the essays of Genius and a laudable cultivation of the Arts and Sciences, which had begun to flourish in so eminent a degree, before the hand of oppression was stretched over our devoted Country."[8] Dwight took great pride in this endorsement, since Washington would be enthroned beside Calvin in the Federalist-Congregationalist pantheon. When Parson's brigade joined the main army at White Plains, Washington further honored Dwight with flattering personal attentions. In his later years, Dwight reminisced with Yale students, a bit extravagantly, about these encounters with Washington, and routinely invoked his name when shouting down democracy. But, despite Washington's auspices, and the efforts of Nathan Hale to obtain subscribers, the poem lay unpublished until 1785. In 1783 Joel Barlow explained that what delayed the publication was Dwight's fear that "some ungenerous Printer will immediately seize upon his labors" and, by making a cheap edition, "undersell the Author & defraud him of his property." [9] If Dwight had anticipated a heavy sale, he was destined to be disappointed.

Dwight's marriage, his wartime experiences, and his meetings with Washington figure less in the poem, however, than do Homer, Milton, and the Bible. Dwight knew Homer firsthand, but it was from Pope that he drew his battle scenes. Like Pope, he extensively copied the Miltonic manner and tone in heroic couplets. He brings many of his epic characters onstage with some variation of Milton's celebrated picture of Satan at the opening of Book Two: "High in the van exalted Irad strode." Much of his syntax is Miltonic, with such Miltonic touches as "intermingled sighs" and "amaze" for "amazement." The structure as well as the language of *The Conquest of Canäan* is Miltonic. Dwight's consultation of the leaders of Israel parallels Milton's infernal council. After Milton, Dwight uses pictures of morning and evening to indicate the passage of time, and in much of Milton's language and order of imagery. From Milton derives the vision of the future from a high hill, the invocation of divine sources of knowledge, the high converse, the summary of world history, the angel messengers, and much more.

Dwight was not the only American poet of his time to borrow widely from Milton. Many poets quoted or adapted Adam and Eve's morning song; Freneau, James Ralph, and many others lifted Milton's hilltop vision of the future.[10] No less conventional was Dwight's treatment of biblical subject matter. The allegory-like device of narrating American history in terms of biblical parallels was common and traditional, flourishing in the colonies uninterruptedly since the Puritans. To the few American readers of the time conversant with native poetry, or to the many who attended colonial commencement exercises, *The Conquest of Canäan* must have sounded like an anthology of set-pieces, an elaborate treatment of some popular conventions.

The Bible also served Dwight as a model for the varied and animated verse he wished to write. Like the Puritans, he regarded the Bible as in part a literary work. Puritans cited biblical precedent to justify their writing of elegies and verse anagrams; Dwight turned to the Bible to justify his epic poem. While working on the first draft, he delivered a commencement "Dissertation on the History, Eloquence, and Poetry of the Bible," published in 1772. In it he attacked the Classical "rules" by arguing the superiority of biblical poets, and he made clear his preference for the simplicity of Paul, the "natural, unstudied language of affection," [11] over the artificial eloquence of Demosthenes or Cicero.

Like many others in his time, Dwight tried to explain literary character by environment. The Jewish or "Eastern Genius," he said, differed from the Greek or Roman because of the climate in which the biblical writers lived. The "vivifying rays of the Sun" (presumably absent from Greece) inspired them to bold metaphors, lively descriptions, and passionate exclamations. Later, when foreign critics claimed that the wilds of America bred savage inhabitants, Dwight flatly denied any association between climate and race. Now, however, he explained to his audience that from the Bible's greater liveliness could be learned the art of engaging and holding the reader's attention.

Dwight admired the animating devices of Scripture: by prosopopeia, forests sing, winds praise, Goodness talks, and thus "awaken our lethargic inclination . . . put in motion the vis inertiae of our constitution." He praised the biblical writers for engaging the reader by actions "new, sublime and wonderful," especially divine interpositions. He was particularly impressed by the Bible's dramatic treatment of history: it never merely tells us who did what; rather "we see them; we hear them speak." Instead of generalizations, it offers the reader a "clear, distinct, and perfect idea of any transaction" by means of "an exact relation of every minute, important circumstance" (surely a misrepresentation of the Bible's very sparing use of detail). Its final and most important means of holding the reader's attention, Dwight felt, was by variety. It presents many differing verse forms—odes, pastorals, satires, elegies, epics—many, differing incidents, many, differing characters, each one—Moses the legislator, Joshua the general, Solomon the prince —a source of amusement and instruction.

Before seeing how Dwight applied these tactics to his biblical epic, it should be added that in his "Dissertation" he called not wholly justified attention to the freshness of his subject. He affected to draw new narrative principles from the Bible, to defy brashly the critic "who doubts whether he may eat, or breathe, unless by *Aristotle's* rules." But, despite his eurekan tone, he was enlisting in a war that had waged in England for fifty years.[12] Even a generation before Dwight's address, many English critics were more disposed to praise Milton for breaking the rules than to argue that the genres were immutably fixed. After 1750, many freely criticized Virgil for lack of invention, saying he merely imitated Homer; many freely criticized Homer for displaying barbarous manners. Dwight's disdain for the "rules" and his loose definition of epic as "simple narrative" were hardly unique.

Actually, much of what Dwight professed to discover in the Bible derives from Lord Kames. Kames also stressed the importance of capturing the reader's attention by presenting particulars over generalities and by stirring him to quick perceptions of beauty or sublimity. Dwight could claim some originality for applying Kames's principles to the Bible, since neither he nor his audience had as yet seen Bishop Lowth's *De Sacra Poesi Hebraeorum* (English translation, 1793), which similarly treated the Bible as poetry. Much else derives from the Yale library. Milton, for instance, had also argued the superiority of Hebrew to Classical poetry; and Dryden had said that the epic should illustrate various ideals of ethical conduct. The real novelty of the "Dissertation" lay in Dwight's choice of a literary topic for a Yale commencement, suggesting the changes he and Trumbull had wrought in the curriculum.

Dwight's mockery of "Critical Manacles" was merely fashionable. It is no surprise, then, that in his own epic, he did everything he could to avoid breaking the "rules." He casually tortured the biblical narrative into obedience with the Classical unities. In his preface to the epic he announced having altered the order of the scriptural battles to make the battle of Gibeon climax the whole. He announced having transferred all the action to the neighborhood of Ai, for unity of place, and having telescoped a campaign of many weeks into the single activity of a few days, for unity of time. To further conform the Bible to Aristotle, he rid himself of unpromising scriptural characters and invented new ones. Dwight's treacherous Hanniel, second only to Joshua, is barely mentioned in the Bible, where none of the heathen leaders has any prominence. He invented a host of women characters and Joshua's protégé Irad, a portrait of himself. Far from emulating the inspired waywardness of "Eastern Genius," he deliberately imposed on the biblical text a crude symmetry. He balanced the Canaanite lovers Elam and Mina by the invented Israelite lovers Irad and Selima, Joshua by the Canaanite hero Jabin, the beginning and end of each book by a description of day or night. Lest the reader miss the shape, he appended footnotes spelling out the parallelisms.

Dwight did, on the other hand, emulate the "animation" of "Eastern Genius," largely by prosopopeia. In wishing to imbue all nature with action, he described so many thunderstorms that Trumbull suggested he supply a lightning rod with the poem. Dwight's definition of epic as "simple narrative" and his admiration for the "natural" language of Paul were theoretical. In his own epic he followed Kames's idea of amplification, producing grandeur through reiterated impressions and rhetorical fireworks; and the poem owes to the theory of reiteration its repetitiousness. The droning sameness of Dwight's battle scenes results from an extraordinarily small range of diction and from an obsession with a few rhymes. As in "America," he particularly likes to rhyme "skies-rise" and "main-plain." With a few slight variants he repeats them hundreds of times; within sixty lines of Book Three (819-84), he rhymes "the plain-their train," "dreadful plain-hopes again," "darkening train-heap'd the plain," "burst amain-along the plain," "driving rain-o'er the plain," "obscuring rain-homeward plain," and "wreath to gain-skirmish'd plain." In the last book alone, "skies" is rhymed with "rise" twenty times, not to mention numerous "skies-cries," "skies-surprise," and so on. In describing the dozens of battles he forswears invention: he allows every lance to "hiss," spill each enemy's "vital tide," and invariably "stain" the field with the invariable "purple gore."

The verse, too, lacks variety. Everything happens in one unvarying, metronomic rhythm. "Animation" meant to Dwight simply an orgastic accretion of storm-tossed oceans, earthquakes, tempests, thunder, trembling heavens, whirlwinds, gales, blood-red skies, and hosts of murmuring widows. By prosopopeia each banal detail takes on the bombastic sublimity of nature:

> As when two seas, by winds together hurl'd,
> With bursting fury shake the solid world;
> Waves pil'd o'er waves, the watery mountains rise,
> And foam, and roar, and rage, against the skies:
> So join'd the combat; ranks, o'er ranks impell'd,
> Swell'd the hoarse tumult of the hideous field;
> Black drifts of dust becloud the gloomy ground;
> Hoarse groans ascend, and clashing arms resound.
> And now, where Zimri broke th'embodied war,
> Imperious Hoham drove his sounding car;
> Like flames, his rapid courses rush'd along,
> Forc'd a red path, and crush'd the thickening throng. . .
> (XI, 717-28)

Under the weight of thousands of such lines, Dwight smothered the narrative clarity and the "natural" language he wished to reproduce; and he tired the attention he wished to engage.

The dramatic treatment Dwight professed to admire in the Bible also suffers from his repetitiousness. The action, bloated by "animation," lacks moment. Nothing can be seen or heard through the curtain of rhetoric. Dwight made no dramatic distinctions. The characters share the narrator's idiom. Men and women, youths and sages, heroes and villains, discourse in the same rhythm, the same diction; and all seem to be saying the same thing. Worse, Dwight provided no quotation marks to sever dialogue from narrative. One sometimes cannot tell whether the narrator or some character is speaking; and, if some character, which one. Borne on the flood of bombast, the reader often does not feel the unprepared and inexplicable shifts in point-of-view, which Dwight often planted in the middle of a verse paragraph, unmarked by punctuation or by changes of tone or rhythm. The repetitiousness serves to disguise the otherwise glaring mismanagement of the action, and the result is by turns tiresome and bewildering.

Dwight's insensitive handling of climactic moments is, however, less damaging than his addition to the completed poem of Books Three and Five, the romance of Irad and Selima. He masked the irrelevance of this sentimental subplot by involving his lovers in a half-dozen harrowing skirmishes, written in the sublime style, and padded with didactic asides on art and nature, and a tribute to Benjamin West. The interlarded subplot robbed the poem of its already enfeebled dramatic point. For, incomprehensibly, Dwight failed to adjust the existent plot to the newly inserted matter. Originally, the first three books depicted the Israelite camp as apprehensive and gloomy at the prospect of battling a superior enemy. But, between Books Two and Three, Dwight interposed the first account of his lovers. So, in the final text, Book Three closes with the Israelites exultant, "Their hopes new-kindled, and their terror gone"; bewilderingly, Book Four opens, the very next morning, when "In every face suspense and grief appeared." This same book ends with the slaying of a kidnapped Israelite youth and with a picture of his delirious father returning the corpse amidst "weeping warriors." Originally, and reasonably, this led into renewed war preparations in the Israelite camp. But, between the delirious father and the war preparations, Dwight inserted a further book on Irad and Selima. In the completed version, the delirious father is succeeded by Selima and "untroubled Irad" strolling on the plain conversing about the visible heavens.

Ironically, Dwight thus reverted to the iconoclasm of his "Dissertation," wrecking the unities he had fought to preserve in defiance of his own theories. Regarding the technique of the poem, at least, one does not quarrel with Henry Adams' view that on Dwight "almost every other mental gift had been conferred in fuller measure than poetical genius." [13]

III *The Allegory*

Dwight apologized in his preface for choosing "a subject, in which his countrymen had no national interest." Yet most of his contemporaries read the poem as an allegory of the Revolution, with Washington represented by Joshua. "America is obviously placed before us," an English reviewer said, "under the allegory of the Israelites having left Egypt, which means the British government." [14] This interpretation irked Dwight. In a letter to Noah Webster he denied any allegorical intent. He conceded a resemblance between the American and Israelite causes, and between Washington and Joshua, "great & good Characters acting at the head of armies, & regulating the chief interests of their countrymen." But he insisted that, first, it was unlikely "that a youth of 19 should conceive & execute so tedious & unpleasing a task, as an Allegory of such extent"; next, that all the essential parts of the poem, including the portrayal of Joshua, were written before the war began; and, decisively, that it was absurd to imagine "the *Conquest* of a country a proper event, under which to allegorize the d*efence* of another country." [15]

Dwight was not telling the whole truth. First, he liked allegory, particularly scriptural. Next, he was far from finishing his epic before the war began. The author of the published poem was not a youth of nineteen but a public figure nearing thirty-five. Decisively but ineptly, he did try to use the "*Conquest* of a country" to allegorize "the *defence* of another country"; and his addition of "by *Joshua*" to the title he submitted for Washington's patronage suggests that he had the parallel in mind. His wish to dedicate the poem to Washington, moreover, reflects a nationalistic demand for historical art by a public proud of its recent glorious past and eager to commemorate it. That public read the past allegorically anyway. Certain that one could learn from history, anxious to create symbols of their revolutionary beliefs, conscious that their every act was potentially representative and set a precedent for future behavior, they employed history as an ideological weapon.

In the arts of Revolutionary America, history became a vehicle of political philosophy and partisanship. The past became a metaphor of the future. In idealized tableaus and statues, artists wrought visual symbols of such republican ideals as Liberty, Science, and Freedom masquerading as Roman matrons or as Classical orators. Biblical vehicles were even more popular and more expressive, for they recalled that treatment of American affairs in the guise of biblical narrative which had been maintained in the colonies since the Puritans, to whom the story of the flight from Egypt seemed a glowingly meaningful type of their own migration to the new world. During the Revolution, these traditional parallels gained a new life.[16] The division of the Red Sea became a nearly obligatory comparison for the rout of the British armies, or for dissent within the American ranks. Trumbull, for one, described the Whigs who "roll'd in either side in arch/ Like Red Sea waves in Israel's march."

Indeed, the likening of Washington to Joshua was a commonplace. By anastomasia, the rhetorical figure which identifies character traits with historical personages, the Puritans dubbed such favorite leaders as John Winthrop or Thomas Shepard, "Joshua." Later, any leader sufficiently brave could be Joshua: Ezra Stiles called Washington "American Joshua"; in *M'Fingal,* General Clinton appears as "British Joshua." The Revolutionary writers revived the Puritan figure, and few men of the period were emotionally and intellectually so closely in touch with Puritan ways as Dwight himself. His mother, Jonathan Edwards' daughter, encouraged him before he was ten to read the historical parts of the Bible, as well as Josephus and the modern histories of the Jews. In his early verse he attempted to retell important sections of the Bible. The stories of Esther and Daniel spoke intimately to his frame of mind, and no doubt seemed to him vibrant with personal and social meanings.

And Dwight joined other Revolutionary preachers in defending the American cause on scriptural grounds. In a sermon written shortly after his appointment as chaplain to Parson's brigade, he showed how the current war "exceedingly resembles that, between JUDEA and ASSYRIA. The cause of both was the same. HEZEKIAH paid a tribute to SENNACHERIB, and these States to GEORGE the third; but in both instances insatiable tyranny demanded more than the tributaries were willing or able to pay; this was the cause." [17] He then squeezed from an ingenious but labored reading of Joel minute points of comparison between the biblical situation and the present—so many, in fact, that Putnam refused to believe that such a text existed in the Bible, and charged Dwight with manufacturing it for the occasion of Burgoyne's defeat. (Dwight himself later regretted the piece and thought it trifling.)

In short, a biblical poem on a patriotic theme would have been no novelty in Revolutionary America, or in America at any time since 1630. Dwight probably did intend writing a patriotic allegory. His disavowal is probably owing to the fact that he later inserted the irrelevant romance of Irad and Selima, and that he intermittently dropped and renewed his design of matching the American and Israelite causes, as the biblical narrative allowed.

Where the scriptural action did not allow Dwight to allegorize the Revolution, he managed to link the two by similes. The death of each Israelite chief in the poem calls forth an heroic apostrophe to a distantly related patriot. Dwight compares the dead youth Aram, for instance, to the "bright and generous" Nathan Hale, his former student. Through these apostrophes Dwight introduced into his biblical paraphrase a summary of the American argument for Independence, as in his tribute to "gallant Mercer," fallen at Princeton:

> When first his native realm her sons decreed,
> In slavery's chains, with want and woe to bleed,
> Check'd, through his bosom fond remembrance ran,
> The cause of freedom was the cause of man.
> In that fair cause he bar'd his manly breast,
> The friend, the hope, the champion, of th' oppress'd.
> (VIII, 455-60)

Dwight included apostrophes also to Joseph Warren, to Major Andre, and to Generals David Wooster and Richard Montgomery. Each one combines an affecting tableau with a flat statement of republican principles, while keeping the similarities between the Israelite and American causes always in view.

Even if he intended no exact parallel, Dwight imagined Joshua in the same terms in which his contemporaries imagined Washington. If Dwight's Joshua does not convey the historical Washington, he does convey the folk hero whose commanding mien and noble character, whose guidance of an army destined to win freedom, were glorified in the poems of Philip Freneau and the Connecticut Wits, in the epics of Richard Snowden and John Blair Linn, and in countless popular songs and ballads, works whose recurrent epithets were duty, fortitude, patience, modesty, politeness, and resolution, making the essence of Washington his sobriety.

In his own "Discourse on Washington," delivered in 1800 and published together with the "Farewell Address," Dwight drew an elaborate parallelism between Washington and Moses. The resemblance, he said, is "so evident, that the recital of it is become almost proverbial."[18] He distinguished Washington's character from that of such chiefs as Alexander, Caesar, and Genghis Khan, as being unmixed with inhumanity. Accordingly, Joshua in Dwight's epic is a study in humaneness; for Dwight significantly changed the Old Testament account to allow Joshua to display compassion.

The biblical Joshua leads Israel in stoning and burning Achan and his family; Dwight's Joshua has only Achan die, and shows him pity. The biblical Joshua commands his captains to stand on the necks of the five Amorite kings, then kill them in cold blood; Dwight has the kings killed in fair battle. When the Canaanites trap Joshua's detractor, the worthless Hanniel, Dwight has the forgiving Joshua rescue him. By contrast, the Canaanite leaders in Dwight's poem are fiendish. One preserves a sword spattered with "purple gore," fondling it in his tent with "fierce transport," exulting how "their gor'd children bleeding parents view." Dwight describes the warfare of the *Conquest* as a manichean struggle between the humane and the vicious; and Washington represents the mild manners Dwight wished to see around him in New England.

Next to Washington's humanity, Dwight admired his practical temper and clear judgment. "Perhaps there never was a mind," he wrote in his "Discourse on Washington," "on which theoretical speculations had less influence, and decisions of common sense more." His highest praise for the historical Washington was that "Whatever passions he felt, they rarely appeared," while in "the most hazardous situations, no man ever saw his countenance change." He admired that marmorean Washington of Gilbert Stuart's portraits, the heatless serenity bordering on emptiness. In the poem, Joshua's comparable sobriety is summed up in his advice to the Israelites: "each gay prospect scan with searching eye." He warns his followers that "Life's a long solitude, an unknown gloom." Beneath Joshua's Augustan eloquence and purple robes stirs the unhappy Calvinist, ever mindful of limitation.

Dwight often insists on Joshua's healthy respect for practice over theory, reason over passion. What fits Joshua for leadership is not his political vision but his exemplary family life, for he extends the tried methods of domestic government to the whole nation: "At once his friends, his race, his Maker, serv'd;/At once his own domestic bliss preserv'd;/ In nice dependence rang'd the servant train,/And o'er his house bade beauteous order reign" (IV, 373-76). Like Dwight's Washington, the military genius of Dwight's Joshua consists not in desperate sallies but in levelheaded plans that enable him to capitalize on the enemy's "childish rage." The climax of the poem occurs in Book Eleven, when "Joshua by a stratagem draws the Heathens from their advantageous post." Like the

Washington of the "Discourse," Joshua is a teacher whose self-governance, reverence for God, and sobriety set a precedent for American character and teach the nation how to rule. In portraying Joshua, Dwight was drawing, if not the historical Washington, The Ideal Republican Leader. The Washington of his "Discourse" was as much an idealized figure as the Joshua of his poem. Whether or not Dwight intended an allegory, Joshua represents what men like Dwight wanted Washington to be.

Dwight comes closest to identifying the Israelite and American causes in the debate between Joshua and Hanniel in Book One. Their argument over whether the Israelites should return to Egypt allegorizes the patriot and loyalist attitudes toward Independence. Secretly jealous of Joshua, Hanniel addresses the disheartened Israelite tribes with "dissembled woe." While pleading for reason, he subtly hints at Joshua's faults, hoping to undermine his authority. He implies that Joshua is quixotically too rash and too cautious, that he is motivated by pride, and that the starved, bedraggled Israelites persevere against a powerful enemy only to feed Joshua's ego. The Israelites' dissatisfaction with Egyptian rule, he says, was prideful; to punish it, God has withdrawn his favor. He bids the Israelites abandon their "unbless'd purpose" and return to Egypt-England, where "robes of kings succeed this garb of woe." (Dwight's graduating class, it might be noted, voted to appear for their degrees in homespun.)

Hanniel justifies his preference for the "robes of kings" by listing the advantages of monarchy, and the disadvantages of independence. Regal trappings enhance authority. Without "decent show," power would grow weak; base minds would think it feeble. Tribute is justified because the crown will protect Israel-America from the imperial designs of other nations, and from internal dissension: "who share the blessing must the tax supply." On the other hand, independence is expensive and politically dangerous. An independent, untaxed Israel would have to support its own military establishment. Deprived of the knowhow of a superior culture, its "arts" would decay; its lands grow wild: "Those realms what culturing hand shall teach to bloom?" Loosed from the empire, its government would founder: "What system'd rule the union'd tribes obey?" The disparate tribes could be united only at the cost of faction, or of tyranny. Assuring the host that Egypt desires their return, Hanniel urges retreat.

The crowd, "with airy visions fir'd," now listens to Joshua. His reply recalls the Washington of Dwight's "Discourse": "Perhaps there never was a mind, on which theoretical speculations had less influence, and decisions of common sense more." Joshua warns the host to distrust utopias: "each gay prospect scan with searching eye." Against Hanniel's glib promise of "robes of kings," Joshua offers, "with dignity sublime," a difficult victory and the fulfillment of an historic mission. Whatever Hanniel's theory, the purely practical consequences of returning to Egypt must be disastrous.

History, Joshua sees, empirically exposes the failure of monarchical rule: "Scarce can each age a single king confess,/Who knew to govern, or who wish'd to bless." Returned to Egypt, Israelite children, sharing the corruptible nature of men, would copy Egypt's corrupt manners and debased worship. In the prosperity of its alien minority, an envious Egypt would see its own ruin, and would seek revenge against Israel. Return to, not flight from, Egypt would turn heaven against Israel, for failing to fulfill its errand, "To found an empire, and to rule a world." Those who with Hanniel argue retreat, Joshua believes, want only to feast and loll in Egypt, escaping a difficult messianic destiny. Joshua for the moment sounds startlingly like Michael Wigglesworth upbraiding New England a century earlier: "For this dire end, were such bright scenes bestow'd?/For this, th'eternal covenant seal'd by God?/For this did ocean's trembling waves divide" (I, 681-83). Finally, Joshua answers Hanniel's doubts that the disparate Israelite tribes can unite without faction or tyranny. Despite sectional differences, he sees the Israelite-Americans inspired by a single character, a communal will:

> By friendship's ties, religion's bands combin'd,
> By birth united, and by interest join'd,
> In the same view our every wish conspires,
> One spirit actuates, and one genius fires;
> Plain, generous manners vigorous limbs confess,
> And vigorous minds to freedom ardent press . . .
>
> (I, 725-30)

To this vigor and plainness, the "decent show" of monarchy is repugnant and humiliating.

Although Dwight protested that the conquest of one country could not allegorize the defense of another, Canaan in the poem clearly represents an idealized America. In July, 1776, Dwight delivered a "Valedictory Address" in which he summarized the nation's political and natural advantages. He emphasized that the "great fact" of the new nation was its uniformity. One religion, one language, a single set of manners, and a communal will bound together the vast, otherwise diverse continent. While other empires began in ignorance and superstition, he explained that America emerged when men "learned to despise the shackles of custom, and the chains of authority" and when "every science is handled with a candor, fairness and manliness of reasoning which no other age could ever boast."[19] In temporal terms, he saw America as the last stage of the westward march of empire, as "the last retreat of science, of freedom and of glory." In spiritual terms, he viewed it as the threshold of the millennium, where "the progress of temporal things towards perfection will undoubtedly be finished."

The America Dwight thus described to his undergraduates reappears in Joshua's Miltonic vision of futurity in Book Ten of *The Conquest of Canäan.* The same Joshua who warns the Israelites to "scan each gay prospect" delivers a rising glory poem with its own gay prospect of the ideal future. Suddenly the sad Calvinist becomes the commencement patriot. Dwight renders much of Joshua's vision in terms of conventional nature—a prophecy of "spacious plains," valleys, and gardens—and in terms of iron, gold, and gems, the vision of America as the Western Ind celebrated by Elizabethan voyagers, where "warm'd by happy suns, gay mines unfold,/The useful iron, and the lasting gold." Otherwise, like the America of Dwight's "Valedictory Address," Joshua's Canaan is informed by a single will, where "union'd Choice shall form a rule divine." It too will be founded in an enlightened, progressive era, "unlike all former realms by war that stood." It too represents a culmination of secular and religious history, "The last retreat for poor, oppress'd mankind!":

> Then lofty towers in golden pomp arise;
> Then spiry cities meet auspicious skies:
> The soul on Wisdom's wing sublimely soar,
> New virtues cherish, and new truths explore:
> Thro' time's long tract our name celestial run,
> Climb in the east, and circle with the sun . . .
>
> (I, 765-70)

Neither in his epic nor in his "Valedictory Address" does Dwight found this immense promise upon a purely secular theory of history. What determines the nation's destiny is not its character or will, nor the inevitable cycles of history, but a providential God bestowing divine favors. Like Joshua, this God sometimes acts as a Calvinist skeptical of "gay prospects," and sometimes as a commencement orator sharing the ideals of Revolutionary Americans. He promises Joshua:

> . . . Thy chosen hand
> Shall guide my sons, and rule that promis'd land.
> That land, where peace, and every pleasure reigns,
> O'er heaven-topp'd hills, and fair, extended plains;
> Where countless nations build the lofty dome,
> Nurse purpling vines, and teach the vales to bloom;
> That land is thine. . . .
>
> (II, 739-45)

Dwight's God was a nationalist. Only He could offer so resplendent a future to the unrenowned heroes and unimposing achievements of a yet unnamed country. Wishing to celebrate America, but finding little tangible to celebrate, Dwight claimed Canaan and Joshua as archetypes of America and its leaders.

For all its optimistic visions, Dwight's epic betrays signs of cultural confusion and uncertainty about the actual aims of the new republic. Throughout the poem contend the differing expectations of Dwight the minister and Dwight the patriot. The poem's gory sublimity detracts from its portrait of Joshua's humaneness and from its hope that enlightened America will be "Unlike all former realms by war that stood." It also violates Dwight's personal and lifelong abhorrence of war. At Parson's camp he attended prisoners sentenced to death, and never forgot seeing a bonfire used to cremate bones, and parts of bodies floating in a pond filled with corpses. The rationalist Dwight who preached progress, benevolence, and peace, who condemned the *Iliad* as barbaric, contested with the epic poet who needed a heroic national subject.

One way in which Dwight tried to harmonize the two was by depicting the Israelites as gentle and heroic at once. What prevents them from battling is not only exhaustion or a wish to return to Egypt but their gentle natures. Joshua and his host are innocent and reluctant killers. In taking his first life, young Irad reminds one of Natty Bumppo in James Fenimore Cooper's *Deerslayer,* or of Robert Jordan in Ernest Hemingway's *For Whom the Bell Tolls,* of that mingled innocence and violence at the center of American life:

> When first his arm, immingling in the strife,
> Drew the red stream, and spilt a human life,
> (A lovely youth oppos'd his hapless head,
> And with pure crimson died the infant blade)
> Thro' his chill'd veins a new, strange horror ran
> And half-form'd tears in either eye began;
> In his young heart, unus'd to create woe,
> Instinctive sympathy began to glow;
> The dreadful scene he gaz'd, and shook to hear
> The hollow groan and see pale death so near.
> (VI, 347-56)

At other times, however, this benevolent strain in Dwight bows to the demands of the epic poet. When Selima, Irad's fiancée, argues against slaughtering the Canaanites because of the other young lovers and innocent children in their camp, Irad answers that those babes and sweethearts will mature into adepts of sodomy, incest, and depravity: "Should then these infants to dread manhood rise,/What unheard crimes would smoke thro' earth and skies!" (III, 275-76). They should be killed, Irad urges, while young, sparing the world their evil and glorifying the Almighty: "Thus God be witness'd sin's unchanging foe."

As the feelings of Dwight's heroes fluctuate between reasoned benevolence and pious butchery, the God who directs them appears alternately as a fearsome Yahweh, "sin's unchanging foe," and an Augustan painter of nature who exquisitely "wakes the beauties of the vernal morn." Faintly but constantly Dwight's conviction of man's sinfulness registers its distrust of his enlightened belief in progress and reason. His Revolutionary optimism was tempered from the first by his belief in human frailty. His pompous visions of American grandeur alternate with quiet calls for restraint. The ideal of an America freed of custom and authority, enjoying edenic innocence, defending the rights of man, is undermined by Joshua's sober advice to "scan each gay prospect," his sense that "laws only claim a righteous sway," his anti-utopian view that the Israelites had better:

Trust no gay, golden doom, from anguish free,
Nor wish the laws of Heaven revers'd for thee.
Survey the peopled world; thy soul shall find
Woes, ceaseless woes, ordain'd for poor mankind.
Life's a long solitude, an unknown gloom,
Clos'd by the silence of the dreary tomb.

(IX, 601-6)

While Joshua first prophesies progress and Augustan splendor, then warns against man's limitation and inherent evil, the glory of America foreseen in Book Ten is questioned by the doomsday vision that directly follows it, reminding one that worldly glory is frail and will be broken down.

Dwight could not decide whether the foundation of America's greatness would be the restraints it imposed on human nature, or the restraints it broke. In his early poems he contrived varying accounts of the American past suited to one view or the other. *The Conquest of Canäan* depicts prehistoric America as a blooming Eden; "America" calls it a "desart." Also, the two poems ascribe contrasting motives to the first settlers. In the *Conquest* " 'Tis virtue prompts, and GOD directs the way." In the more secular "America," settlers come "Forc'd from the pleasures of their native soil,/Where Liberty had lighten'd every toil." Uncertain whether America was a liberation of the spirit or a test of its endurance, Dwight devised differing accounts of the Atlantic crossing as well. In "America" the trip to the "desart" is a cruel trial: "Th'unfathom'd ocean, roll'd in mighty storms,/Want and Disease in all their dreadful forms." But in the *Conquest,* where America usually appears as Eden, the crossing is serene: "No dangers fright; no ills the course delay." In part, these differences arise from perceiving America as a past or a future event. In the *Conquest,* Dwight wanted to give Joshua a sense of the resplendent future ahead; in "America," he wanted to give his contemporaries a sense of the difficult past overcome. But less superficially these varying senses of the past express the conflicting beliefs of Dwight the patriot and Dwight the minister.

Indeed, Dwight submitted yet a third version of the American past in "Columbia," a popular song he composed in 1777 and published six years later. Wholly secular, "Columbia" admits no fear that America is a transitory event in the unfolding of God's plan; until the final lines its optimism is unqualified. While

"America" imagines the new nation as an event in European history, while the *Conquest* regards it as a motion of God's will, "Columbia" denies it any ancestry whatever. It no longer has an English, or any, past; it exists apart from history: "Columbia, Columbia, to glory arise,/The Queen of the world, and child of the skies!" [20] As a "child of the skies," America need not insure its future by the achievements of its past, or found them on God's favors; and the poem's vision of the future is correspondingly vague: ". . . that empire shall rise,/Extend with the main, and dissolve with the skies." But Dwight restrained even these nebulous hopes. In the last stanza of "Columbia" he unexpectedly manufactured a gloom-ridden narrator, straying down a lonely valley, away from "war's dread confusion" in the contemporary scene. The somber present weighs heavily on the ideal future and brings the "child of the skies" down to earth.

For the rest of his life, political realities would toss Dwight, quite maddeningly, between acting as the champion of man's illimitable progress and acting as the scourge of man's infamous nature.

IV *Reaction*

The discordant versions of America in *The Conquest of Canäan* and in Dwight's shorter poems of the period not only reveal Dwight's ineptitude or his wavering feelings; they dramatize again the problems of being an American writer in Dwight's time. No national audience existed for a poem on an American theme; and, if Dwight wrote about what he knew, the Connecticut Valley, he was likely to seem parochial or obscure, not only in England but in other sections of America. The alternative was vagueness, banality, and wholesale imitation of English writers. Through the quasi-allegory of the *Conquest,* Dwight was addressing both his own situation and an unfamiliar public.

The sizable, and largely hostile, critical response to *The Conquest of Canäan,* illustrates Dwight's predicament. William Cowper blamed Dwight for being both too traditional and too personal. On the one hand, he attributed what he found forcible in the language to Dwight's imitation of Pope. But where Dwight struck out on his own, Cowper found him cryptic and outlandish. He criticized his "Transatlantic English" and his apostrophes to American "heroes." He objected to the mysterious respect accorded "a Mr. Warren, who fell in battle at Charlestown; and . . . a Mr. Mercer, who shared a similar fate at Princeton."[21] Another English reviewer patronized Dwight's effort as "a promising blossom of polite literature sprung up on the American continent." Regarded as a provincial branch of European poetry, he thought it passable; as a uniquely American poem, he thought it muddled, narrow, and dull. "Our American epic," he complained, is "exceedingly void of interest to any readers, except such Americans as may perceive their country and their late war allegorized under the name of Canaan."[22]

Significantly, the same local materials that in England seemed interesting only to Americans, in America went unnoticed. Here the poem was widely read but unenthusiastically received. Although advertised for sale as far away as North Carolina, and although extracted in numerous periodicals and quoted in such works as William Dunlap's *Father* and William Hill Brown's *Power of Sympathy,* it was looked upon mainly as another, however splendid, Augustan poem. Noah Webster saw Dwight as rivaling Milton, Homer, and Tasso, and as preparing for the day when "unborn Dwights adorn th' Augustan age."[23] Unfortunately for Dwight, his epic appeared at the same time as Barlow's more clearly topical *Vision of Columbus,* with which it was often unfavorably compared, no doubt feeding Dwight's growing hatred of Barlow. One American reader, who contrasted the contemporary relevance of the two poems, decided that had Dwight's "cost as much labour in the building, as an Egyptian Pyramid, it is as useless a work, and will like it remain only a monument of the labour it cost the builder."[24] Barlow himself generously saluted "daring" Dwight in his *Vision* and, almost alone, appreciated his intent: "His voice divine revives the promised land,/ The Heaven-taught Leader and the chosen band./ In Hanniel's fate, proud faction finds her doom. . . ."[25] But, on the whole, neither fish nor fowl, neither scriptural narrative nor Revolutionary epic, Dwight's poem proved too local for English readers and too remote for American.

Later critics who tried to explain the cool reception of the *Conquest* pointed to the atmosphere prevailing after the Revolution. Joseph Dennie, for one, remembered in 1799 that Dwight "wrote under numberless disadvantages and published at a period, inauspicious to Quiet and Poetry."[26] In his old age Dwight, who adopted this view himself, credited the critics' indifference or hostility to rampant Infidelity after the war. But when the poem first appeared, he attributed its poor reception to its novelty. Shortly after the first reviews he wrote, in self-defense, "The Critics," comparing his detractors to the dogs of Cynethe, Greece. As usual he did not publish the poem for another six years. Drawing on the manner of Pope's "Epistle to Dr. Arbuthnot," he recounted the legend of some vicious, resident dogs who drove away an innocent newcomer by ruthless censure: "A mere barbarian, Indian whelp! / How clownish, countryish, sounds his yelp!"[27] As an "Indian whelp," his epic was, Dwight apparently felt, too American in subject and too crude in technique for English taste.

Dwight also felt that the critics had maligned his originality and had been affronted by his bold defiance of critical "rules":

> But chief, when *modest young beginners,*
> 'Gainst *critic laws,* by *nature* sinners,
> Peep out in verse, and dare to run,
> Thro' towns and villages your own,
> Hunt them. . . .

Actually, no one blamed Dwight for breaking the "rules," which in any case he did everything to preserve. The fact is that by 1785 epic poetry was in disfavor in English critical theory, and even a new English epic might have met abuse. Dwight closed his poem allowing the dog-critics to vaunt their hatred of the "lofty, beauteous, new, and great," among which he seemingly classified *The Conquest of Canäan.* Perhaps what most of all produced his bitterness toward the critics was the lofty view the *"modest young beginner"* of thirty-five took of his accomplishment.

But the reviewers' failure to value the novelty of his epic still grieved Dwight. In 1786 he devoted an installment of his essay series, "The Friend," to justifying the form of *The Conquest of Canäan.* He regretted how the pleasure the reader might take in new experiences is inhibited by past prejudices and precedents. Had Aristotle read not Homer and Sophocles, but Milton and Shakespeare, a chorus would be thought absurd, all tragedies would need five acts, and the *Iliad* and the *Aeneid* would be thought false epics. Then an epic, he insisted, need not resemble the *Odyssey* or *Paradise Lost*: "epic signifies merely narrative."[28] Anticipating *Greenfield Hill,* which he had begun writing, he added that pastoral poetry has also erroneously been defined by the examples of Theocritus and Virgil. All scenes of rural life should be admitted as pastoral subjects. He objected to how narrow generic definitions deprive poet and reader both of new kinds of pleasure, and how poems, "by the manner of forming them, are necessitated to be stale and trite."

Again Dwight's professed contempt for the "rules" stems from Kames, who also thought the ancient critics amiss in elevating a single poem into a class. Dwight's plea for looser definitions of the genres seems partly a retrospective defense of the slipshod technique of his epic (he later reversed his stand and urged poets to follow Aristotle rather than nature) and partly a lament that his career was doomed by stupid and un-American deference to authorities. He closed by hoping that in America "so much independence of mind will be assumed by us as to shake off these rusty shackles, examine things on the plan of nature and evidence, and laugh at the grey-bearded decisions of doting authority." His hope was uncalled for, since no one in America seems to have thought the poem novel. If his allusions to "a Mr. Mercer" displeased English readers by their parochialism, they failed to strike American readers because of their infrequency.

Yet there was justice in Dwight's view of the novelty of the poem. One does sense an underlying, if aborted, design—the ghostly promise, as in much early American verse, of some new kind of poem which failed to materialize. Roy Harvey Pearce has said that the basic style of the American epic "is to make a poem which will create rather than celebrate a hero and which will make rather than recall the history that surrounds him. In the American epic what is mythified is the total milieu and ambiance, what the poet takes to be the informing spirit of his time and his world."[29] The real theme of *The Conquest of Canäan* is its tone. Its subject is a desired sensibility. It is a true epic in the one sense that its manner, if not its theme, is deeply rooted in national beliefs and desires.

Like many other poets and painters of the period, Dwight translated into the events of ancient history an ideal of American character, a sense of the personality appropriate to republicans. To be an American, he and others felt, was to have new feelings; and he filled his poem with unembodied but representative emotional states, with postures usually declaring benevolence plus courage, reason plus endurance, democracy plus righteousness. Joshua and his host comprise a model ruler and a model ruling class; and all are conscious, as was Washington, of their exemplary roles. Their actions, like the congressional debates over the proper manner of addressing the President, reflect the self-consciousness of young America, its awareness that its every sentiment, every procedure, tested whether it would remain a republic or would lapse into monarchism. No more precise embodiment of the aspirations of Dwight's place and time exists than the poem's shocking insertion into cosmic battles between good and evil of paeans to "a Mr. Warren, who fell in battle at Charlestown," its juxtaposition of Joshua and Nathan Hale, Canaan and Ridgefield Hill, innocence and brutal glory. These disconnections record an America whose promised greatness was deeply felt to be incommensurate with its actual accomplishments, an undramatic culture which yet claimed a momentous heritage and wished to be understood only in terms of a still more glorious future.

The American epic, Pearce concludes, "is not *about* history; it *is* history—the history of men pondering what it might mean to be heroic enough to make history."[30] But Dwight knew precisely what it meant to "make history," and he felt that America would make it. The true hero of the poem is Dwight himself, the history-maker, his culture's representative man. The poem is intended to show that a country largely wilderness could produce such a poem, that ten years after a great war it could call forth such noble feelings at such length in language of such sublimity, and that its homely ways could inspire in one of its citizens such consequential feelings. Nearly the most important part of the poem is the understated avowal of Dwight's preface that expresses his wish to throw "in his mite, for the advancement of the refined arts, on this side of the Atlantic." *The Conquest of Canäan* is a gesture of cultural maturity. It celebrates itself.

CHAPTER 2

The Possible America

I "*Ten thousand follies through Columbia spread*"

UNEXPECTEDLY, events during the last years of the Revolution severely shook Dwight's nationalistic faith. His optimism for the country's future, his belief in the wisdom of Independence, already weakened by his Calvinistic sense of ingrained evil and his insistence on habit and custom, faltered under personal setbacks and the moral failures of the newborn republic.

In October, 1778, Dwight's personal ambitions collapsed. While with the main army at White Plains, he received news of his father's death, forcing his return to Northampton. The elder Dwight, who had ventured up the Mississippi River to Natchez, had intended to found with his sons a Connecticut-type settlement. But he died of a fever; Dwight's brothers were robbed by Indians, then hunted by Spaniards who stole the title papers to the land. His father's death burdened the idealistic, twenty-six-year-old Dwight with support of his twelve brothers and sisters, his mother, plus his own young wife and infant son. In addition, upon his return he had to contend with the animosity of all Northampton. His father, refusing to fight on either side of the war, had gone to Natchez to escape it. So among the same neighbors who had driven his grandfather, Jonathan Edwards, out of his pulpit, Dwight now lived under the stigma of Toryism. One of his brothers went insane after being shot at by local patriots, who burned the Dwight fields and scattered the oxen.

As he always could, Dwight exerted himself to redress fortune. He sold some of his father's three thousand acres, labored in the fields on his two farms, ran a school, preached at parishes as far away as Boston, and managed to support the large family. He more than won back the town's respect: in 1781-82 he served as its representative in the state legislature, and he was even nominated as a candidate for the Continental Congress. He could have entered national politics but said he could not make the inevitable sacrifice of principles for party. Instead, his exhausting labors having improved the family's situation, he accepted in November, 1783, a ministerial call to the rural parish of Greenfield Hill, in Fairfield, Connecticut. Northampton had left him little time to further his literary career. Under the settled regime at Greenfield Hill, however, happy with his salary of five hundred dollars a year, he again worked at becoming "our American poet."

But Dwight's voice had turned strident. He appraised the national possibilities with sour circumspection. In an outpouring of poems, essays, and sermons, he diagnosed infidelism, democracy, and dandyism as symptoms of national moral rot. And he traced them, *radix malorum,* to Europe. In an "Epistle . . . to Col. Humphreys," written upon David Humphreys' voyage to Europe in 1785 (but unpublished until 1795), he borrowed the irritated manner of Pope's imitations of Horace to discharge his disgust at continued American dependence on Europe. Against the "sunny genius" of the republic, where man is "Phoenix divine," he posed that "dy'd serpent," that "tinsell'd out-side," that "painted tomb," "that foul harlot, Europe."[1]

Dwight warned the embarking Humphreys that young Americans who for improvement wander to "custom's shrine," too willingly exchange happiness for splendor, truth for art. Their "plain, frank manners," their manly republicanism are violated and corrupted:

> Train'd in foul stews, impoison'd by the stage,
> Hoyl'd into gaming, Keyser'd into age,
> To smooth hypocrisy by Stanhope led,
> To truth an alien, and to virtue dead,
> Swoln with an English butcher's sour disdain
> Or to a fribble dwindled from a man.

Dwight observed that, returned home, the Europeanized American thinks himself great and demands homage for the fashionable but poisonous views he condescendingly imparts to his witless countrymen:

> A prodigy his parts; an oracle his tongue,
> Hist! hist! ye mere Americans, attend;
> Ope wide your mouths; your knees in homage bend;

> While Curl discloses to the raptur'd view
> What Peter, Paul, and Moses, never knew;
> The light of new-born wisdom sheds abroad,
> And adds a leanto to the word of God.

This "travell'd Ape," unmoved by the moral implications of Independence, believing that wisdom is "on Atlantic travellers breath'd by heaven," has at the same time missed the practical knowledge, the "Commercial wisdom," he might have gained by staying home. Dwight pleaded that Humphreys, while in Europe, guide himself by native common sense and manliness and steer clear of speculation and fancy manners by remaining "all Columbian."

This venom toward a contagiously corrupt Old World gives Dwight's work a new tone. It expresses his concern that the Revolution, far from creating a spirit of personal independence, had resulted in a more slavish subservience to Europe. In 1786 he wrote two new installments of "The Friend" essays in the persona of a cultured swain, "John Homely." Homely's name suggests both his humility and his jingoism. Contemptuously he reports hearing a farmer ask his "dada" should he plow a certain field. This reminds him of certain Americans inhibited, still, by "an infantine dependence upon Great Britain."[2] (After his father's death, it may be worth noting, Dwight turned repeatedly, in fact and metaphor, to relations between fathers and sons.) Americans, Homely frowns, conspire in prolonging their babyhood, and in earning the contempt of foreigners, by adopting a European view of themselves as inferiors. Uncritically, they acknowledge what Europeans allege, that everything in America is a degenerate, "Creolian" branch of the superior stock.

Dwight bristled particularly at one form of this cultural vassalage, the special favor accorded recent immigrants. Americans, Homely says, think every European a man of genius. Indignantly he cites an Irish tallow chandler who upon setting foot in America was made a solicitor general. In every one of his earlier poems, Dwight saw America as the "last refuge of poor, oppress'd mankind." But now he invoked his theory of motives to warn against a too favorable treatment of immigrants. "It is a trite, but important maxim of common sense," Homely claims, "that the mind is wholly influenced by motives."[3] No motives, no activity. Dwight believed that the great motives of property, influence, and reputation excite a spirit of emulation by which a society thrives. And in America he saw this formula for progress rendered inoperable by the craven preference shown Europeans. Disheartened by the unmerited success of immigrants, native Americans lose their ambition. By extending their own advantages to Europe, they promote their own loss, and are to blame for their low esteem abroad: "To respect ourselves, is the first advance towards the respect of others."

America's self-destructive attachment to Europe was not the only threat Dwight saw to the new republic. He found his ideal of a single America united in conduct and sentiment imperiled by parochialism and faction. The Revolution had doubly failed his hopes by producing a fawning dependence abroad and a defiance of national authority at home. Like many others in his time who sought some national principle or institution that could wield authority, he felt that the greatest defect in the government was its lack of coercive powers; and he pressed the exercise of the implied powers of Congress to coerce the states. In an essay on "the judgment of history concerning America" (1787), he listed the virtues of the Revolutionary generation, as future generations might see them: its passionate love of liberty, its hatred of "strides of arbitrary power," its inspired obedience, its spirit of union and "virtuous exertion."[4]

But he mourned how the colonies, united in danger, came apart in peace. Selfish passions asserted themselves until, without European meddling, there arose "disunited councils and opposing measures, ingratitude to their benefactors, injustice, cruelty and oppression, contempt of government and laws, human and divine disaffection, distrust and jealousy with a numberless train of follies and vices, and, at length, the flames of a civil war were kindled, and—what follows let historians record." "Liberty" had gone too far for Dwight, producing faction and threatening disunion.

In the same year, Dwight recast this Wigglesworthian warning against dissension into a poem to the then convening Congress, "Address of the genius of Columbia to the members of the continental convention." Still reluctant to give up his idealized America, he had his swain-like "genius of Columbia" submit to the Congress a familiar vision of America as the home of freedom, science, and virtue; as "the last recesses of oppress'd mankind"; and as the immense transcontinental empire, thronged by a "gen'rous race" of natural men united in faith, politics, and language:

> Chain'd to no party; by no system bound;
> Confining merit to no speck of ground;
> Nor Britons, Frenchmen, Germans, Swiss, or Huns,
> Of earth the natives, and of heav'n the sons,
> Regarding, loving, all the great and good,
> Of ev'ry rank, clime, party, sect and blood.[5]

But to this vision of universal brotherhood, John Homely's jingoism and contempt for immigrants gave little encouragement.

The "Homely" side of Dwight would win out. Dwight came to feel uncomfortable not only among foreigners, but soon doubted that he could share a single country with anarchic Westerners, slave-holding Southerners, Old-Light theologians, Jeffersonians, Illuminists, and Deists. Even in the "Address" Dwight saw his ideal of union shaken by postwar factional bickering and local rebellions: "Ten thousand follies through Columbia spread;/Ten thousand wars her darling realms invade."/The private int'rest of each jealous state;/Of rule th'impatience, and of law the hate. But, clinging to his ideal hopes, he discounted the present difficulties by optimistic rhetoric. The "ten thousand follies" abroad in America reflect, somehow, the machinations of a "few base wretches" who "mingle gen'ral woe." Although "rule, unsystem'd, drives the mind astray," and although "private int'rest points the downward way," he instructed the Congress not to despair of "freedom, glory, bliss." He urged it to build national feeling by rejecting "each colonial aim," and by speaking continentally, not as "the small agents of a paltry town."

To aid Congress in realizing the country's promise, Dwight set out at length and in closed couplets the differing responsibilities of the states and the federal government. He recommended what had already been generally accepted as needed changes in the Articles of Confederation: the states should control taxes, justice, private rights, and aid for religion (a vital point for Dwight); but commerce, war, treaties, should be administered federally. Above all, he wished the Congress to be prepared to enforce its laws: "Persuasive dictates realms will ne'er obey:/Sway, uncoercive, is the shade of sway." Unlike the younger Dwight who had sneered at the "shackles of custom," the "genius of Columbia" praises

Time because it "Habituates men by law and right to live;/To grey-hair'd rules increasing rev'rence draws. . . ." This respect for "grey-hair'd rules" refutes the wisdom of the epic poet who derided "the grey-bearded decisions of doting authority," and of the benevolent Joshua who appealed to his divided tribes by reason alone. Yet the poem ends with a vision of futurity foreseeing a "chosen race" peopling "stupendous realms," bridging Dwight's wishes and his doubts by ignoring their conflict.

II *The Scope and Technique of* Greenfield Hill

To supply a new, less poeticized model for American character and government, Dwight began writing, in 1787, his long pastoral poem, *Greenfield Hill.* As usual, his other activities interrupted, and the poem was being written off and on until its publication in 1794. Beginning to win a national reputation as a preacher (although his ever weaker sight limited him to extemporaneous sermons), he entered national church affairs with a plan to promote a general union among Presbyterian congregations. Besides grooming his fields and gardens for relaxation, by raising rare plants he became one of the first Americans to cultivate strawberries; and, by experimenting with the soil, he discovered a way of killing the lice that destroyed his watermelon vines. In between, he managed to publish *The Conquest of Canäan* and a few short poems. He indulged his genuine and lifelong fondness for society by numerous visits to New York to talk poetry with his brother-in-law William Dunlap, and by entertaining frequently at his large white house at Greenfield Hill, between Long Island Sound and the fields and forests of Connecticut.

This house and its adjacent lands are the scene of *Greenfield Hill,* its metaphor for society, and its reason for being. The property dominates the poem. Although Dwight declared in his preface that he wrote "aiming merely to amuse his own mind and to gain a temporary relief from the pressure of melancholy," he loved the place and wished to honor its style of life; and this style becomes a living example of what America can be. Dedicated to John Adams, *Greenfield Hill* is one product of the lively contemporary debate on whether the people could govern themselves and, if so, how. During the Confederation, the nature of government was a subject of inexhaustible popular interest. While in public meetings, newspapers, and conversation Americans tried to explain, justify, or denounce what the continental convention had done, Dwight, who hated theory, presented Greenfield Hill as an existent utopia, the great good place achieved, the inevitable model for governing the nation at large.

The poem consists of seven sections. As the following summary makes clear, Dwight intended to imitate in each section a different English poet, in the manner of William Mason's *Museus,* an ambition he only half-realized:

1. "The Prospect" (Thomsonian blank verse). Standing atop Greenfield Hill, the narrator describes the surrounding countryside at harvest time. He recalls the recent war, and contrasts British invaders with American troops, adding fervent wishes for peace. He surveys and praises the society and manners of Connecticut as against those of Europe, and exhorts Americans not to imitate European ways. Finally, he describes the happy lot of the rural clergyman, and urges the clergy to lead humble lives and to call mankind to virtue.

2. "The Flourishing Village" (heroic couplets, imitative of Goldsmith's "The Deserted Village"). The narrator describes the village in winter and spring. He lists the pleasures of rural life in America, contrasted with the pomp and squalor of Europe. He explains how the local situation could be further improved by eliminating slavery, which he discusses in its American and West Indian forms. He extolls the unique virtues of the New England church and school, the manners of women and patterns of female society in Connecticut. These suggest a general comparison between the "improving state of society" at Greenfield Hill and the social stagnation of Europe. Finally the narrator praises the Western migrations.

3. "The Burning of Fairfield" (octosyllabic couplets, with frequent imitations of John Dyer). The narrator recounts the British sack of the New Haven vicinity in July, 1779. His detailed descriptions of the burning of local houses and the misery of the people lead to a general condemnation of war, and of the idea of the hero. After a speech by Death, the narrator counsels America to avoid war.

4. "The Destruction of the Pequods" (Spenserian stanzas, with imitations of James Beattie's "The Minstrel"). A local mother relates Mason's defense against the Pequods, emphasizing the ro-

mantic possibilities of the subject. Her narrative prompts reflections on the nature of the Indians, on change, and on the inevitable collapse of empires.

5. "The Clergyman's Advice to the Villagers" (octosyllabic couplets). A clergyman, on his deathbed, discourses to his parishioners on sin, virtue, the value of the present life, the means of salvation, public worship, family religion, and charity. The sentimental aspect of the scene is pronounced. He depicts a parochial clergyman's life and deeds, and dies.

6. "The Farmer's Advice to the Villagers" (octosyllabic couplets, with echoes of Benjamin Franklin's "Father Abraham's Speech"). A farmer addresses to some assembled villagers a string of moral aphorisms, and some related tips on farming and husbandry. He recommends to them an industrious and economical life, and the advantages of social harmony. He tells them how to educate their children, stressing the supreme importance of habit.

7. "The Vision" (heroic couplets). The "Genius of the Sound" now appeals not to Greenfield Hill but to all America. He contrasts America with ancient empires and contemporary despotisms. He discourses grandiloquently on nature in America, the division of property, penal policy, the promotion of national arts and sciences, the American clergy, American manners and, finally, America's mission in the world.

Such an outline perhaps suggests that Dwight had enlarged his poetic ambitions to deal with a new variety of subjects and with greater technical daring. On the contrary, *Greenfield Hill* reexamines in a pastoral setting the issues of *The Conquest of Canäan*. Like the epic, it is preoccupied with war, with society, and with America's destiny. And its seven contrasting parts, its frequent interjections and set-pieces, serve the same demand for variety which Dwight earlier prescribed as an essential means of holding the reader's attention. Dwight also reworked the method and materials of his epic in particulars, for the same adulatory apostrophes to American heroes appear in Part Four of *Greenfield Hill,* where John Eliot, Samuel Stone, John Norton and other Puritan worthies emerge as victims of Indian brutality and as exemplars of colonial hardiness. The same handful of swollen, cosmic epithets Dwight applied to the epic combat now render the battles of Fairfield and the Pequod wars: "host with host" is still engaged in "combat's ridgy van" under "tempestuous" skies, with the same obsessed rhyming of "trains-plains" and "rise-skies." While these battle-pieces still delight Dwight as opportunities for rhetorical salvos, their dramatic force is improved by the octosyllabic couplets, which create a headlong narrative energy, missing from the *Conquest,* that is suitable to the strife. Moreover, nurtured in the tradition-minded society of Northampton, Dwight knew the French wars as a source of still living grief to his friends and relatives. His interest in battle often turns from a wearisome exploitation of gore to war as a reality of consciousness. The nightmare past is shown in the scarred present, and it offers lessons for the future.

While practicing his ideal variety, Dwight strove to relate the seven parts of the poem to a dominant action and to give them a clearly narrative form. The preface places the narrator atop Greenfield Hill, and the succession of prospects from that point of view theoretically determines and orders the subjects of the poem: "The First object, there offering itself to his view, is the Landscape; which is accordingly made the governing subject of the First Part of the Poem. The flourishing and happy condition of the Inhabitants very naturally suggested itself next."[6] Despite Dwight's good intentions, these connections are usually slight. The idealized landscape has no vital relation to the more realistically treated condition of the inhabitants. The prospect justifies the content only when, observing the Pequod Swamp, the narrator reminisces about the Pequod wars.

Otherwise, the hill device does not draw together the loose medley of themes. Often Dwight tries to defend a glaring digression by reinvoking the hill in a guilty parenthesis—" (From yon small field these meditations grow)"—or by main force: "From these fair scenes, to wonders more refin'd. . . ." Yet even in his preface he apologizes for the "mixed manner" of the poem, and indeed his prefatory remarks on the hill device have the desperately affirmative air of an afterthought. The succession of prospects is often broken by unrelated vignettes—The House of Sloth, The Female Visit, The Indian Character—some of which Dwight later published as independent poems. One feels that he included them in *Greenfield Hill* only to salvage some yet unpublished verses.

Dwight could have given the poem a sort of unity in variety by his several imitations of British poets. Instead, many of the voices say the same things and blur the differences they were meant to create. Like the *Conquest, Greenfield Hill* suffers from an insensitive repetition of themes and phrases. Dwight was incapable of holding in mind the larger design. The "Arguments" to the various parts are often indistinguishable: "the happy state of the inhabitants" (Part One), "Description of a happy village" (Part Five), "the happiness of America" (Part Seven). What in theory justifies this redundance is that each part of the poem sees the subject from a slightly different point of view and through a different set of conventions, depending on the writer imitated. But whether the language recalls Goldsmith, Beattie, or Franklin the same happy village shows through.

The hill on which the narrator stands is less a narrative device, however, than the symbol of an intense localism. Whether sketching ideal types, commemorating historic personages, or recounting battles, Dwight's interest is in Greenfield Hill, in telling its past, prophesying its future, and assessing its present. The point is worth repeating that Dwight believed more deeply than anything else what he quoted from William Penn:

> Nothing is necessary to make good men harmonious and friendly but that they should live near to each other, and converse often, kindly, and freely, with each other.[7]

Dwight's intense localism, his sense of the richness and value of the local scene, his *pietas,* orders the poem. The complementary first and last parts—"The Prospect" and "The Vision"—frame a deliberately balanced picture of the local past, present, and future, of what Greenfield Hill is, how it came to be, and how it may be maintained. The first two parts depict the present state of society; parts Three and Four explore the past; parts Five and Six explain how the present state of happiness may be preserved; Part Seven, on the basis of the rest, prophesies the future. The two parts within each division complement each other. Part One offers a prospect of the countryside and nature, Part Two a contrasting prospect of the village and society. Part Three presents British atrocities during the recent Revolution, Part Four the contrasting Puritan heroism a hundred years earlier. In Part Five, a clergyman tells how Greenfield Hill's religious life may be maintained; in Part Six a farmer tells how its secular prosperity may be maintained. And this interest in local history, not the fraudulent "prospect" device, unifies the poem.

Dwight's commitment through forty-five hundred lines to a parochial scene was an act of daring unprecedented in any earlier American poem. Partly, the times forced Dwight to be daring by making him question his ideal, but vague, America. Fleeing from a nation subservient to Europe and marked by internal dissension, he became the celebrant of a state. And this gave his poetry a new actuality. As his vision of American greatness shrank, he felt less willing to write sonorous rhetoric as a testimony of American genius. *Greenfield Hill* marks, therefore, a new concreteness in Dwight's style. The poem's abundance of place-names—"Grover's beauteous rise," "Mill-hill," "Norwalk's white-ascending spires"—gives the diction some freshness and vigor. What affords the final vision of futurity is not "Columbia," but a local deity, the "Genius of the Sound."

To speak with even this degree of intimacy to his situation, Dwight needed to create a new audience. No longer writing for all America, he specifies that the group of established farmers he is addressing occupy "about thirteen square miles. On this little tract were found, at the time of the late census, almost fourteen hundred inhabitants." Accordingly, the poem's standard of social and personal good is the life Dwight lived at Greenfield Hill at the time. Within its narrow focus the poem presents a complex and detailed account of town life, its ideal shape and practical shape, its manners, conduct, polity, its mode of preserving the past. *Greenfield Hill* precedes Emily Dickinson's Amherst, as well as E. A. Robinson's Tilbury Town, Edgar Lee Masters' Spoon River, and Sherwood Anderson's Winesburg as the first delineation in American literature of the township ideal: "every town/A world within itself."

Not only this localism organizes the poem, but also Dwight's continual unfolding of the "glorious contrast" between Europe and America. Standing on Greenfield Hill, between Long Island Sound and the fields of Connecticut, the narrator mediates between the Old World and the New. The fourteen hundred inhabitants, Dwight notes, are proportionately "a population as great, as that of Britain," thus a fair contrast to it. Politically and morally unwilling to continue glamourizing the whole of America, Dwight discovered in the very shrinkage of his subject the means for rivaling Europe's literature. He seized on Greenfield Hill as a real foil to Windsor Forest, a real place with a real past and real prospects:

> Etherial! matchless! Such as Albion's sons,
> Could Albion's isle an equal prospect boast,
> In all the harmony of numerous song,
> Had tun'd to rapture, and o'er Cooper's hill,
> And Windsor's beauteous forest, high uprais'd.
>
> (I, 12-16)

Beside the resplendent youth and innocence of Greenfield Hill, Europe seems a "bad world," a "world unclean," lost in outworn creeds and superstitions, a "Garment gothic, worn to frittering shreds," its historical cycles alternating between eras of butchery and of stagnation. In Europe:

> . . . heavy drags the sluggish car of time;
> The world unalter'd by the change of years,
> Age after age, the same dull aspect wears;
> On the bold mind the weight of system spread,
> Resistless lies, a cumbrous load of lead . . .
>
> (II, 654-58)

This omnipresent "glorious contrast" between Europe and America further augments the solidity of Dwight's language by calling forth descriptions both of the local scene and of its European counterpart. Dwight's abhorrence of European vices and his fear lest they spread to America, elicited from him specific accounts of European manners. The "glorious contrast" released him from the vague optimism of his earlier verse. By showing him America's actual possibilities and limitations, it sharpened simultaneously his diction and his politics. It drew the realistic Calvinist into the rhetorical domain of "our American poet." Dwight, who required a sense of danger, always wrote best with an enemy in view.

In finding Greenfield Hill the equal of Cooper's Hill, however, Dwight still implicitly acknowledged Cooper's Hill as the standard of social good and vernal beauty. This standard the poem both adopts and disowns. As a European standard, Dwight dismisses it as mere unrealized pipedreaming; as a Connecticut standard, he lauds it as an existing fact. It was the agony of colonial literary life, the constant strain of writing in a borrowed culture, that

Dwight was always forced to criticize the conventions that allowed him to see. The very writers he imitates he expressly deplores. Pope, whom he copies at length, he finds offensive: to any person "of delicacy, and virtue," "The Rape of the Lock" contains "several lines plainly indelicate, and some grossly obscene"; "Eloisa to Abelard" displays sentiments "gross and noxious"; and the "Moral Essays" and "Satires" trespass "against truth, justice and decency." Addison offends in the same way.

Yet Dwight anticipates the time when America will produce its own Pope and Addison: "Another Pope inchanting themes rehearse,/Nor the meek virgin blush to hear the verse;/Improv'd, and clouded with no courtly stain,/A whiter page than Addison's remain" (VII, 489-92). The very culture Dwight loathed gave him the only terms he knew in which to express his hopes. Because his borrowed language bound him to an English view of his situation, his terms of praise for Connecticut are the conventions and poetic images of a culture that in his view has "prostituted" them "to the celebration of vile characters, to the display of subjects and sentiments gross and pernicious, and to the commemoration of facts, which deeply stain the name of man." Tied to images and conventions he considered meretricious, Dwight tried to overcome his dilemma by envisioning America in *Greenfield Hill* as a sort of purged Europe, where for the first time poetic conventions became realities.

Dwight's several imitations of British writers are not, then, wholly stylistic exercises; for manner interests him less than matter. His sources supply the image of Europe for his "glorious contrast." In the "distinguished writers" of England, he finds and parades unflattering descriptions of British society, "warranting all, that is asserted in this poem." English criticism of English life allows him to discover the value of American life. Where Goldsmith writes in "The Deserted Village": "Sweet smiling village, loveliest of the lawn,/Thy sports are fled, and all thy charms withdrawn," Dwight uses the criticism by pointing up the "glorious contrast" in "The Flourishing Village" of Connecticut: "Sweet-smiling village! loveliest of the hills!/How green thy groves!! How pure thy glassy rills!" (II, 73-74). Dwight includes dozens of imitations of Goldsmith, Thomson, John Gay, Beattie, and others; and he supplies the parallel passages in footnotes, expressing his scorn of the culture on which he depended. These imitations amount to a kind of serious parody. They mock England for prostituting the social values which they praise Connecticut for redeeming.

Dwight had begun wrestling, in short, with the problem of an American language. He saw that the new republican personality could not speak in the old European voice. In an "Essay on Language," published in 1810, he remarked that language reflects national character, since *"nations will uniformly have such words, as express those ideas, which they wish to communicate."*[8] Joel Barlow had found in the new republic a subtle divorce between language and thought. In a Fourth of July speech he noted that the "practical tone and tension" of the American mind is incongruent with its abstract principles: "We are like a person conversing in a foreign language, whose idiom is not yet familiar to him."[9] Surely the rhythm and diction of contemporary English verse, particularly its balance and its Classical imagery, were awkward vehicles for the crudely pragmatic, uncosmopolitan society of Greenfield Hill. Visions of an America with "temples starr'd with gems and roof'd with gold" tell what Americans thought they ought to feel and ought to sound like. They are public professions of hopes never inwardly felt. In *Greenfield Hill* Dwight tried to break through these public abstractions. Forced to deal with the local scene, he was also obliged to forge a language suitable to the "practical tone and tension of our minds."

Toward creating such a language Dwight introduced into *Greenfield Hill* dozens of regional usages and Americanisms. In conjunction with local place-names and the names of local heroes, these create a distinctive idiom. The use of nativisms, as well as the detailed glosses Dwight supplied for them in his footnotes, was not unprecedented in colonial verse. For instance, in a pastoral poem on Maryland, Jonathan Boucher had italicized and glossed thirty-odd Americanisms; Ebenezer Cooke, in "The Sot-weed Factor," had introduced and annotated many more. Both poets, however, addressed their glosses to English readers as examples of colonial queerness and vulgarity. Dwight addressed his to Americans outside New England as examples of local color, and as explanations of novel manners and institutions.

Dwight introduced into the poem five types of new language. A first group of words merely dignifies the humble subjects of pastoral: the Connecticut River appears as "Connecta," the Mississippi as "Louis" (recalling its relation to Louis XIV). A second group consists of localisms which Dwight expanded for the sake of making himself understood outside of the local scene:

> Lawrence (n.): A proverbial name, in some parts of New England, for a lazy person.
> Fit the Ground: A customary phrase, in some parts of New England, to denote the preparatory cultivation of a field, which is to be sown.
> The Post: It is customary, in New England, when property is taken by distress, to advertise the sale of it upon a post, erected for that purpose.
> Townman: In New England, the prudentials of each town are commonly placed under the direction of a small number of men, chosen for that purpose, and called indifferently selectmen or townmen.
> Member of the house: A representative; Vulgarly called a member of the house.

A third group contains dialect words defunct in England, but revived in the common speech of New England: "Slump'd" ("to denote the sudden sinking of the foot in the earth"); "Streets" ("the roads through the villages are called streets"); "wain" for wagon or cart. A fourth group consists of pure Americanisms, the names of new things: "spring bird," "Nutwood," "Indian wind" (hurricane), "India's curse" (rum). Lastly, Dwight glossed some words fairly common in English literary speech—"sheen," "sere"—which he apparently felt would puzzle his local audience.

The poem's indebtedness to its English models is, of course, immense; yet *Greenfield Hill* was the first lengthy poem in America so consciously written for a native audience, the first to so consciously resist sounding like British English. No other colonial poem, except the propaganda verse of the Revolution, has a native audience so much in mind. Dwight's appropriation of the local scene compelled him to assemble place-names, unfamiliar proper nouns, and Americanisms to form a rudimentary American literary speech, stilted, hesitant, and incomplete, but recognizably not British.

Dwight created not a single literary speech, but, more accurately, a number of native voices. The seven parts of the poem employ as many local personae, secondary narrators introduced by the narrator on the hill: a rural minister, a farmer, a parochial schoolmaster, a local mother, the "Genius of the Sound." These voices echo Dwight's varied roles at Greenfield Hill as preacher, farmer, teacher, father. He enhanced the dramatic distinction between these voices by metrical variety. Unlike *The Conquest of Canäan*, *Greenfield Hill* allows each speaker his own pulse—blank verse, heroic couplets, octosyllabics, Spenserian stanzas—and his own idiom, depending on the British writer imitated. Each persona, moreover, assumes a different perspective on America and on the village. From the minister's point of view, America is the site of the millennium, while the farmer sees it as a verdant Eden; accordingly, America appears as "New Canaan" or "New Albion" or "Western Albion" or "Columbia." The variety of voices offered Dwight a way out of his uncertainties. It enabled him to test out various attitudes toward America without being pledged to any one of them.

Dwight's own voice is most often found in the prosy sociology of the footnotes. *Greenfield Hill* is both a poem and an essay, for Dwight included fourteen pages of closely printed notes (not a few of which apply to the wrong lines). The notes contain much of the most interesting matter in the work. Dwight perhaps thought these candid appraisals of the local scene not lofty enough for verse. Or, more likely, he was reluctant to subject them to his borrowed language and form for fear of compromising their honesty. He often uses his wealth of commentary (there are footnotes to the footnotes) to question the "poetic" claims of his own narrator. The notes specify, state limits, offer statistics, facts, degrees of truth. Their direct, unliterary language establishes within the poem a dialogue between rhetoric and actuality that suggests Dwight's new awareness of the difference between public hopes and practical beliefs.

Greenfield Hill struggles against its own rhetoric. In his divided state of mind Dwight attempted to write a conventional poem that should break through the conventional poetic view of American life. He tried to distinguish between the real bliss of Connecticut and the literary Eden, to discover if in Connecticut "the soul-intrancing scenes,/Poetic fiction boasts, are real all." In doing so he gave his sympathies to facts far more than to "poetry," correcting the fanciful optimism of his epic. Yet, while more circumspect, the result is, like the epic, something between a poem and a tract, half a literary exercise on the glories of American life, half a straightforward account of the mores of the Connecticut Valley, neither a mythic description of ideal conduct nor a treatise on practical government. *Greenfield Hill* asks whether one can write "poetry" about America at all, or only footnotes. Dwight did not answer the question for himself until 1800; then he stopped writing poetry.

III *Society in* Greenfield Hill

This argument between poetry and footnotes embodies a further "glorious contrast" between facts and theories, working governments and utopias. The premise of *Greenfield Hill* is that observably, empirically, the people of Connecticut are the happiest on earth. Dwight insists on their "good, real, pure/With guilt unmingled," their "happy local situation," their "unblemish'd cheerfulness." He brandishes this observed happiness against contrasting utopias, "fairy schemes" which defraud mankind. An investigation of the sources of this felicity, he says in a footnote, "would probably throw more light on the true methods of promoting the interests of mankind, than all the volumes of philosophy which have been written."

Dwight believed that the type of society which produced the real happiness of Connecticut would produce it for the nation. The poem treats untested social theories as "mere dreams" and political philosophers as "mere theorists." It argues that no theory can be complex enough to anticipate practice, although the intellectual pleasure of making systems is so great that men "are still employed in building air-castles, and in seriously expecting to inhabit them." On the other hand, Greenfield Hill is long-evolving, proven, workable, indebted not to French *philosophes* but to the hardheaded forefathers: "The common sense of the early Colonists of New England saw farther into political subjects than all the Philosophers, who have written since the world began." The poem repeatedly offers traditional, native practice in opposition to untested, foreign theory. Undercutting "mere theorists," Dwight cites with quiet defiance a multitude of homely but efficient means of government. In New England, he observes, a parish bell is rung at nine each evening, "a custom, which has more influence in promoting good order, than a slight observer would imagine."

This opposition between the pragmatism of New England and the pipedreams of France restates, without the allegory, Joshua's warning to "scan each gay prospect with a searching eye." Yet, again, Dwight's language and his innate idealism held him to the mere dreams and "gay prospects" he disowned. In *Greenfield Hill* he denounces the ideal while, however, approving its realization. He attacks utopian theories as foolish in every respect but that, in Connecticut alone, they have been realized. Greenfield Hill, an actual Eden, proves "Hesperian fables true, if true, here only." Sometimes the prosy footnotes strain to validate the claims of the "poetry," whose extravagance now made Dwight uncomfortable and apologetic:

> Morose and gloomy persons, and perhaps some others, may think the description too highly coloured. Persons of moderation and candour may possibly think otherwise. In its full extent, the writer supposes it applicable to the best inhabitants only; but he believes the number of these to be great: to others he thinks it partially applicable. Poetical representations are usually esteemed flattering; possibly this is as little so, as most of them. (p. 172)

Dwight still wanted things both ways: in Connecticut, Tritons, Nereids, and the mythology of the east "would find perpetual home,/Were Grecian fables true."

The physical and moral bases of Connecticut's ideal happiness are the hardihood and simplicity of its people. Perhaps because of his own delicate health, Dwight stressed how by enduring a cold and resistant climate the people have grown strong: "Cold is thy clime, but every western blast/Brings health, and life, and vigour on his wings" (I, 92-93). Like the cold climate, the intractable soil makes the people rugged:

> . . . in milder climes
> Their peers effeminate they see, with scorn
> On lazy plains, dissolv'd in putrid sloth,
> And struggling hard for being. Thy rough soil
> Tempts hardy labour, with his sturdy team,
> To turn, with sinewy hand, the stony glebe,
> And call forth every comfort from the mould,
> Unpromising, but kind. . . .
>
> (I, 105-12)

Dwight turned to account whatever facts of Connecticut life challenged his vision of an actual Eden. Such physical liabilities as the cold climate and tough soil, through a law of challenge and response, prove moral assets. Paradoxically, Europeans in more temperate zones are left "struggling hard for being" because they lack challenges. The more demanding climate of Connecticut calls forth an exertion which sinks mountains, spans oceans, fills granaries, and leaves no man a beggar. However stony, the land returns "every comfort." "Unpromising, but kind," it converts every drawback into a pastoral blessing. It serves as both a criticism and a fulfillment of European ideals by showing them as hard-earned realities, not poetic myths: "For here, in truth,/Not in pretence, man is esteem'd as man."

Dwight depicts the manners of this sturdy but comfortable people as simple but elevated. Here too he reproaches European standards while adopting them. Connecticut combines rustic with metropolitan virtues, for simplicity is attained with no loss of refinement and eminence. The people are "great, without pride; familiar, yet refin'd." Dwight illustrates local manners in great detail, compiling what amounts to a conduct-book for parochial life. In suggesting the behavior suitable to the "dignified character of free republicans," his manner is pragmatic and empirical. He lays down few rules, rather describes the practices that have made possible the harmony of Connecticut life. Of special importance is the choice of suitable but unfashionable clothing, making life natural and easy.

Clothing, of course, had great symbolic value for Dwight's contemporaries; for whether Americans could produce their own clothing became a test of independence. In the poem Dwight proposes that as proof of their independence Americans choose and make their garments "with a total superiority to the miserable frippery of artificial society" and reject "all servile imitations of the manners of other countries" as a reversion to colonial status. He warns that the fashions of Europe, particularly of Britain and France, are unsuitable to the climate, convenience, and character of Americans. In a footnote he says he has never seen a woman who "appeared to be so happy, or to behave so easily, as when she was moderately dressed." European women, harnessed in "stiff brocade," fixed in a "studied air," become uncomfortable and mean; and European fashions generally inspire formality, distance, and difficult behavior. Because common sense dictates at Greenfield Hill, people willingly exchange form and parade for sociability and happiness.

Dwight sees in the eighteenth-century preoccupation with

Fashion an argument against rigid class distinctions. He censures "Love spent in looks, and honour lost in words." His scorn of European dress and manners seems squarely based on republican sentiments, but, for himself, curiously, he seems to have favored a beribboned and elaborate apparel. And at times in *Greenfield Hill* the wish that Americans will not copy European dress leads to the admission that they can not. With a majestic sneer at the sour grapes, Dwight notes that the country's "pecuniary circumstances" would be "advantageously consulted, by the adoption of dress, in all respects such as might well consist with our general mediocrity of wealth." He assigns the simple manners of Connecticut now to the climate, now to republican resolve, now to a "general mediocrity of wealth." Significantly, his verse assigns them to weather and patriotism; his footnotes, more often to poverty.

Dwight wrote *Greenfield Hill* during the depression following the Revolution, when from all sides Americans were being asked to exercise self-denial. Since the depression was particularly blamed on English agents and merchants, and on the flood of foreign imports, homeliness and parsimony became nationalistic virtues, living proofs of independence. Dwight went further. He glorified "mediocrity" or "Competence" as the only possible economic basis for the happy society. He reasoned, first, that "mediocrity" insured self-sufficiency and plain manners. Part Six of the poem—a sort of Georgic in which the farmer-narrator provides tips on tilling, manure, pasturage, fuel—describes the "humble joys, to Competence allied"; and it illustrates the dependence of domestic harmony on economic scarcity. Second, Dwight saw in the depression the advantage that it offered few opportunities to vice. Third, he hailed "Competence," like the rocky soil or the cold clime, as a challenge, a spur to progress. Like his Puritan ancestors, he never distinguished between hardship and self-improvement.

"Competence" not only insures plain manners and prevents vice but also guarantees social benevolence and personal courage. While each man has barely enough, it is his own, and thus the society Dwight depicts is both frictionless and individualistic. He addresses "Competence":

> From thee the rich enjoyments round me spring,
> Where every farmer reigns a little king;

Where all to comfort, none to danger, rise;
Where pride finds few, but nature all supplies;
Where peace and sweet civility are seen,
And meek good-neighbourhood endears the green.
Here every class (if classes those we call,
Where one extended class embraces all,
All mingling, as the rainbow's beauty blends,
Unknown where every hue begins or ends)
Each following, each, with uninvidious strife,
Wears every feature of improving life.

(II, 165-76)

The society of "little kings," a republican version of an aristocratic ideal, calls for democratic good will while it preserves a sense of personal authority and power. Its neighborliness and order do not cause stagnation since, in wrestling with the same semi-poverty which creates good will, invention and courage thrive:

Where Competence, in full enjoyment, flows;
Where man least vice, and highest virtue, knows;
Where the mind thrives; strong nerves th'invention string;
And daring Enterprize uplifts his wing....

(VII, 129-32)

Dwight makes "Competence" the "policy sublime" which, having worked in Connecticut, will realize the promised greatness of America. All it needs is for "mediocrity" to be nationally implemented:

. . . alike to want, and wealth, allied,
Plac'd in the mean, 'twixt poverty and pride,
The goal, where faithful virtue most is found,
The goal, where strong temptations least abound,
Nor sloth benumbs, nor luxury betrays,
Nor splendour awes, nor lures to dangerous ways . . .

(VII, 545-50)

By contrast, Dwight locates the evils of European society in its division between too much and too little: "See half a realm one tyrant scarce sustain,/While meagre thousands round him glean the plain." In Europe the poor have no hope; the rich, no motives. "Competence" at once creates and satisfies ambition, and it produces progress without threatening order.

In building his middle-class utopia, Dwight inverted the formula of the Protestant ethic: *less* wealth (up to a point) more virtue. Shabby gentility signifies a lack of pride and ostentation that creates harmony by reducing envy. Dwight overcame his scornful dependence on English verse by using pastoral ideals to attack the pastoral ideal. The goals of Greenfield Hill, like those of Cooper's Hill, are pastoral ease, innocence, and bounty. But they arise from their opposites, a rugged climate, personal hardship, and economic scarcity. So far as the existent, unpastoral impoverishment of Connecticut is the necessary soil for pastoral innocence and bounty, Dwight made his footnotes sustain his "poetry." "Competence" reduced the strain between the patriot looking toward an opulent, powerful America, and the minister wary of luxury and vice.

The ideal "mediocrity" of Greenfield Hill depends on land ownership and on the equal descent of property. These are the legal bases of its happiness. Dwight, like other Federalists, derived from John Locke's *Treatises on Government* a belief in the intimate connection between liberty and the natural right of property. But he expanded on Locke to make property the source also of intelligence and of sound morals, the ally of Christianity in making men behave. Property creates respect for law and, linking self-interest with society, social cohesion. Dwight gave this view, hardly novel in its time, a unique slant by attempting to unite Locke and Calvin and to use property as the social and legal equivalent of a religious establishment. He often insists that the happiness of Greenfield Hill depends upon land ownership. It "undoubtedly arises," he says, "from the equal division of property," from a state of society "in which property descends, by law, in equal shares, to the proprietor's children." He presents the equal division of property as having a double advantage over primogeniture: first, it gives large numbers of men a stake in society, thus motives for acting well: second, it gives no man too much, thus no means for indulging vices.

But conservatism in Dwight, as with the agrarian Southern poets of the 1930's, is never far from pastoralism. Property is a further link between poetry and footnootes, Eden and real estate. To the republican inheritor, a share of innocence and natural joy inevitably comes:

> With flowery brilliance smiles the woodland glade;
> Full teems the soil, and fragrant twines the shade.

> There cheaper fields the numerous household charm,
> And the glad sire gives every son a farm . . .
>
> (II, 689-92)

The land transmits and perpetuates not only the means of existence but also a tone. It keeps alive the frame of mind that would yoke "flowery brilliance" and "cheaper fields." It gives the inheritor a share in the character of the original landholders. It is a legacy of morals and style, keeping alive in each new generation the forebears' discipline, humility, and sensitivity by passing on its historical properties: from private ownership comes independence; from working the resistent soil, hardihood; from having a stake in society, benevolence, love of order, and a self-preservative courage:

> To sons, in equal portions, handed down,
> The sire's bold spirit kindling in the son;
> No tyrant riding o'er th' indignant plain;
> A prince, a king, each independent swain. . .
>
> (VII, 219-22)

Again it is striking that Dwight elaborates his social views in terms of father-son relationships. The transmission of land from father to son became for him a radiant image of the means by which social stability is born and maintained.

In defending the right of property and in condemning Europe for its wealthy few and impoverished many, Dwight does not ignore the problem of slavery in America. But his condemnation of slavery is equivocal. Convinced of its theoretic malignity, he presents its practical workings as benign. The slave he depicts in Part Two is an ancestor of the Happy Darky of later plantation romances: "what voice so gaily fills the wind?/Of care oblivious, whose that laughing mind?" Dwight shows how the harmony and good will imparted by "mediocrity" reach even the slave. Despite his dependence, the slave shares the peace and produce of the system he serves:

> He toils, 'tis true; but shares his master's toil;
> With him, he feeds the herd, and trims the soil;
> Helps to sustain the house, with clothes, and food,
> And takes his portion of the common good. . .
>
> (II, 209-12)

The one deficiency Dwight finds in the slave's life is its lack of freedom: "Lost liberty his sole, peculiar ill,/And fix'd submission to another's will."

Dwight's unperturbed tone is more remarkable for his fervent praise of personal freedom elsewhere in the poem. His pastoral conventions commit him to seeing the slave as a less privileged swain, enjoying the same innocence and harmony as his masters, only more passively. But Dwight's prose does question his "poetry." In a series of footnotes the realist discredits the idyllist by observing that Negro children are "generally sprightly and ingenious, until they become conscious of their slavery" at about age five. Confronted by power and scorn, they wish their condition changed, but find no means. Deprived of praise, esteem, or property, they become cranky and stupid; they drink, and for revenge steal turkeys and horses. Considering the few inducements Negroes have to effort, Dwight says, "we shall more wonder, that there are, among them, so many, than that there are so few, examples of ingenuity and amiableness."

When the poetry indicts slavery as "chief curse, since curses here began" and as "Proud Satan's triumph over lost mankind!," these indictments are leveled against the slave system in Great Britain. Dwight refers the reader, in a note, to evidence taken by a committee of the House of Commons on the barbarous treatment of Africans in the West Indies, and he includes in the poem horrific scenes of West Indian Negroes beaten by ebony canes, hanged from cranes, forced to watch their children's brains dashed out. By means of the "glorious contrast" the evils of slavery in America seem insignificant. The real brutalities of the slave system, Dwight implies, result from and flourish only in a society based on rank and luxury:

> Why shrinks yon slave, with horror, from his meat?
> Heavens! 'tis his flesh, the wretch is whipp'd to eat.
> Why springs the life-blood from that female's throat?
> She sprinkled gravy on a guest's new coat!
>
> (II, 299-302)

Dwight makes slavery, as a form of human brutality, a strictly European vice; in America, it exists as a "peculiar ill," a form of social backwardness. Even then, he notes that in Connecticut, some "interesting and respectable efforts have been made to emancipate the Negro."

Predictably the poem never mentions slavery in the American South. The footnotes, which do mention it, conceive it merely as a hindrance to the national adoption of Connecticut's scheme for happiness. Dwight thought he saw the mild and natural manners of New England spreading across the continent, except to the low country of Virginia and South Carolina, where uniform manners already existed. And Southern manners, he felt, could not persist without the continuance of Negro slavery, "an event, which can scarcely be expected." His cautious attitude toward slavery hints at the delicate posture he was learning to hold, and would continually hold later: defending America against European criticism, while dissociating Connecticut from America so as to also criticize America.

Viewing property as the basis of individual happiness and social harmony, and having observed the country's moral collapse during the closing years of the Revolution, Dwight looks with particular disgust upon war. "The injury, done by war, to the morals of a country," he notes, is "inferior to none of the evils, which it suffers. A century is insufficient to repair the moral waste of a short war." In Part Five, "The Burning of Fairfield," he expresses his horror of war, but almost wholly in terms of property damage. Human death seems to move him less than do the wrack of the "tidy dome" and "glittering spire." He describes little carnage, but "unnumber'd smokes." Each smoldering house signals the ruin of private and civic virtue, of which it is the foundation:

> Unnumber'd smokes began to rise:
> His mansion, long to each endear'd,
> Where peace, and joy, alone appear'd,
> Where all the charities of life,
> Of parents, children, husband, wife,
> With softer, tenderest bosoms strove. . .
>
> (III, 166-71)

Dwight makes the destruction of property the vice uniquely of "Neronian" Europe. Of all the British atrocities at Fairfield he regards none as "more wanton, more useless, and more indicative of the worst character, than burning. No nation, by which it is either allowed, or done, ought to make claim to humanity, or civilization." And, despite their vaunted refinement, he notes, Europeans have waged war seventy-five out of the last ninety-two years because of the same unequal distribution of wealth he condemns as a bar to progress:

> There, in sad realms, of desolating war,
> Fell Despotism ascends his iron car;
> Printed in blood, o'er all the moving throne,
> The motto glows, of—MILLIONS MADE FOR ONE.
> (VII, 287-90)

By "glorious contrast," Connecticut's parents, schoolmasters, and clergymen preach peace and the equal descent of property.

Having damned war in Part Three, Dwight glorifies it in Part Four. While the peace derived from "Competence" satisfied both the wishful visionary and the wary minister, it deprived the epic poet of an ennobling, if bloody, past. In "The Destruction of the Pequods," war, seen in the remote past, hallows the present. It enriches the locale and sets heroic Connecticut beside the great, vanished empires. The narrator of Part Four is a local mother who, relating the Pequod history to her children as a sort of fairy tale, turns war into "poetry." She exalts: ". . . chiefs obscure, but terrible in fight,/Who mock'd each foe, and laugh'd at deadliest harms" (IV, 129-30). The narrator gravely, but bloodlessly, imagines treading "human dust," the remains of some gallant chieftain who performed "deeds sublime" and "soar'd to Caesarean heights, the Phoenix of his age."

Purged of moral complications by its remoteness from the present, the "long-forgotten" war offers a sense of common difficulty overcome that is another bond of social unity. Similarly, in Part Three, Dwight, the defender of property rights, villifies the Hero, instructing him to "Mark thy splendours, whence they rise!/See, on fields, with corses spread,/Thine exulting coursers tread!" (III, 624-26). But, for all this humaneness, in Part Four Dwight becomes once more the epic poet and idolator of Washington, and honors the Hero: "There Mason shone, and there his veterans pour'd./Anew the Hero claim'd the fiends of blood,/While answering storms of arrows round him shower'd" (IV, 236-38). Like Mason, the Indian heroes, even in violent defeat, enlarge the national character, making America the equal in glory of Greece and Rome:

> . . . O ye Chiefs! in yonder starry home,
> Accept the humble tribute of this rhyme.

arbiter of morality. He personifies Thomas Jefferson's ideal gardener who could also play the French horn—the cultured yeoman. Significantly, his account directly precedes the vision of ideal national character in Part Seven; for Dwight wished to make the pedagogic and the cultural goals identical. The farmer mixes his notions of child-rearing and education with tips on husbandry. Their common basis is the self-reliance of an agrarian republic, where literacy and plowing have equal though different importance. His standards are designed to prepare children for the difficult climate, the "mediocrity" of wealth, and the personal freedom they entail. As his mind is pragmatic and realistic, his verse is fittingly spare and direct.

The farmer bids the assembled villagers deny their children everything that creates waste or that fills them with heightened expectations. Instead of "wond'rous stories" and the "pernicious love of fun," he advocates thrift, order, economy, righteousness, and industry. He wishes children to learn to *"reverence righteous sway"*: law, government, country, and the men who created them. At the same time, he wishes to encourage self-reliance, "True independence of our peers," particularly financial independence. While all children must learn how to read, they must also be kept vigorous and healthy. He recommends that boys wrestle and leap, despising "base effem'nancy." By taking pride in competitiveness, by desiring to "win the palm, and prize it, won," they will continue the manliness associated with the land and with the forefathers who passed it on.

Girls must be educated more genteelly, but not less simply. Dwight loathed "fashionable education" for women, whom he considered as capable of mental improvement. The farmer advocates that girls be forbidden novels (which guarantee disillusionment by depicting life falsely), allowed physical exercise, and taught to use the needle and the spinning wheel. Parents must teach them to dress plainly, to be companionable, and to live simple but useful lives. For the sake of progress and social good will, Dwight wished education to be open to both sexes and to all classes. By glorious contrast, the European peasant, deprived of education, lives in perpetual discouragement:

> Hence Education opens, spreading far
> Through the bold yeomanry, that fill thy climes,
> Views more expanded, generous, just, refin'd,

Than other nations know. In other lands,
The mass of man, scarce rais'd above the brutes,
Drags dull the horsemill round of sluggish life;
Nought known, beyond their daily toil; all else
By ignorance' dark curtain hid from sight.

(I, 195-202)

The education the farmer describes aims at producing a variety of "motives." It encourages each republican equally to improve himself, and, like "Competence," promotes progress while reducing envy.

The farmer recites his pedagogic ideals with dogmatic certainty but his account of pedagogic methods is confused. In practice, such an ideal balance between a passive respect for the status quo and cries for independence and progress might be difficult to attain. The local educational problem reflects the national political one of how to grant the states the greatest autonomy while preserving union among them. In his poem to the Congress, Dwight had warned that "Sway, uncoercive, is the shade of sway." But in *Greenfield Hill* he reproves coercion. The farmer regards coercive schooling as a cause of European barbarity and social unrest. Schoolboys taught to respect force doom the nation to constant war, civil dissension, and cultural decline:

From childhood, train'd to wield the iron rod,
Alike regard not man, and fear not GOD.
Science they scorn, the public bar deride;
And every feud by vengeful force decide;
Honour their deity, and will their law,
In private war, the sword of passion draw. . .

(VII, 153-58)

In the farmer's view, social stability is best served by milder methods of discipline. His ideal of guidance without severity might have come from any Puritan treatise on education. The teacher should rule by "influence" and example. He should approve children's interests and contend with their faults in an atmosphere of mutual trust. Teachers and parents, the farmer adds, should be consistent. Their conduct should match their precepts; they should always praise and blame the same things. Furthermore, they should postpone correction until their own resentment and the child's fear subside. In this rational spirit, the child is made aware that "You hate the fault, but love the child."

Yet on the degree of rational example or of blind force needed for effective discipline, Dwight hedges. The poem views children now as "Sweet harmless elves! in Freedom's household born," now as Calvinist mortals rotted by original sin. Reasoning, the farmer indicates, may not be enough:

> Vain hope, by reason's power alone,
> From guilt, no heart was ever won.
> Decent, not good, may reason make him.
> By reason, crimes will ne'er forsake him.
>
> (VI, 417-20)

While elaborately abjuring the rod for discipline, the farmer casually recommends censure, neglect, disgrace, and confinement. Moreover, the "elves" in "Freedom's household" are ruled by habits. Their freedom consists of perfect obedience to perfect inner laws imposed from outside. No form of action, the farmer says, will be of any use to the child unless it is made habitual: *"Habits alone thro' life endure,/Habits alone your child secure"* (VI, 437-38). Dwight's educational views, like his political views since *The Conquest of Canäan,* strike an uneasy balance between freedom and restraint, independence and coercion. The farmer never decides whether men are guilty hearts or harmless elves, whether America is "Freedom's household" or a suburb of "this sin-ruin'd, this apostate world." His self-assured tone outshouts the conflict without resolving it, and suggests how incompletely Dwight had surrendered his youthful idealism.

Restraint would count more for Dwight than release; stability, more than progress. Fearful that local rebellions against national authority would destroy the country, he recommended Habits and "Competence" as homely training for a stable national life. He believed, also, that Habits and "Competence" could preserve society in spite of popular theories about the cyclical nature of history and the rise and inevitable collapse of empires, theories he once shared. In *Greenfield Hill* he developed his own theory, attributing the breakdown of social order not to irresistible cycles, or to divine intervention, but to too great wealth and too much freedom.

The farmer describes how social dissolution occurs in "three descents" that are reminiscent of John Wesley's inexorable chain of piety, virtue, riches, corruption.[11] The farmer postulates that the first generation of Americans are most occupied with earning and saving their money. But soon the patriarch's farms grow; his cattle fatten; and he dresses his sons neatly, sends them to college, builds them a handsome home, and dies. The second generation, born to wealth and ease, but trained in good habits, is ambitious but cautious:

> . . . in those wholesome habits train'd,
> By which his wealth, and weight, were gain'd,
> Bids care in hand with pleasure go,
> And blends oeconomy with show.
>
> (VI, 617-20)

The son keeps a seemly but thrifty house, "Improv'd, but with improvement plain." Prosperous and prominent, he turns to public life; and from townsman he rises to be a member of the House or to be a judge. Fatefully, he consigns the care of his children to his wife; and this removal from private to public life brings social dislocation. The wife struggles to perform duties properly belonging to the husband, then "doubts, desponds, laments, and bends." The sons, bereft of a patriarchal model, "riot, rake, and reign, at home." Finally, the sons usurp their father's place; unrestrained, uneducated, unmastered—but wealthy—they expend themselves on vice. The father may see this, but too late: lands, houses, horses, property are sold or mortgaged. Friendless and broken, the father seeks low company, "Whores, gambles, turns a sot, and dies." His children, in rags, "*pursue him to the tomb.*" The cycle is reversed when the waifs are apprenticed to stern masters. As they re-experience the history of their immigrant grandfather, they learn to toil, again subsist on hard fare, again grow useful.

This wasteful cycle, Dwight felt, could be halted by Habit and "Competence":

> Would you prevent th' allotment hard,
> And fortune's rapid whirl retard,
> *In all your race, industrious care*
> *Attentive plant, and faithful rear;*
> With life, th' important task begin,
> Nor but with life, the task resign;
> *To habit, bid the blessings grow,*
> *Habits alone yield good below.*
>
> (VI, 675-82)

The farmer's account of social change precedes the concluding part of *Greenfield Hill,* a lengthy vision of futurity in which Dwight translates Habit and "Competence" into national terms. As in the farmer's fable of the "three descents," America will sunder its ties with the corrupt European father, emasculated by the "pomp of spoils." Like Habit in the family, "well-system'd rule" in the nation will resist the destructive flux of history. Like the "mediocre" citizen of Greenfield Hill, the nation of small land owners will enjoy equality and permanence:

> See the wide realm in equal shares posses'd!
> How few the rich, or poor! how many bless'd!
> O happy state! the state, by HEAVEN design'd
> To rein, protect, employ, and bless mankind;
> . . . .
> Thrice wretched lands! where, thousands slaves to one,
> Sires know no child, beside the eldest son;
> Men know no rights; no justice nobles know;
> And kings no pleasure, but from subjects' woe.
> (VII, 126-29, 144-47)

In accord with his praise of "Competence" and private property, Dwight gives up the grandiose imperial hopes of his earlier vision poems. He exalts not the immense size or power of America but its impregnable isolation from Europe: "Th' Atlantic's guardian tide repelling far/The jealous terror, and the vengeful war." This isolation is both physical and cultural. For what grants America a splendid future is no longer an Augustan ideal or a gorgeous tone, but the society Dwight described in the homely particularity of its parish curfew bells, through the idiom of its crusty farmers and uncorseted housewives. His spokesman is no longer a "Spirit of Freedom" speaking from a "lonesome vale." It is the "Genius of the Sound" astride Greenfield Hill, naming as augurs of the hopeful future the real though modest accomplishments of the place he stands on.

So far as these hopes were for a stable and pacific America, the achievements of Greenfield Hill sustained them. But Dwight still pined for "Freedom's household," his comfortable housewives still imitated Beattie's minstrel, and at the last he gave in to his rhetoric:

> Then, on the borders of this sapphire plain,
> Shall growing beauties grace my fair domain.

O'er these green hills, and in each smiling dell,
Where elves might haunt, and fays delighted dwell,
From Thames's walks, to Hudson's verdant isles,
See, with fair seats, my lovely margin smiles!

(VII, 615-20)

Dwight finally could not discard his "gay prospect" of a vague, Augustan America. The otherwise cautious "Genius" ends up foreseeing an "aera new of Fame" studded with "Chinesian gardens," "rising bards," and "unrivall'd forms of glory," that are scheduled to appear in what Dwight calls the "fairy hour," although the poem makes abundantly clear his scorn of "fairy states."

Dwight presented the society of Greenfield Hill as a contribution to the contemporary dialogue on the nature of government. He felt that the Revolution he so ardently praised in his epic had failed by creating civil dissension and by not creating cultural independence. In *Greenfield Hill* he tried to show how, over the years and independently of Europe, the New England states had evolved a native and orderly system of government. Its great virtues were stability, plainness, and a sense of the possible. But to these virtues he could still not confine his nationalistic ideals. The courtesy of Greenfield Hill, its manliness, its disdain for luxury, its scorn of "wond'rous stories" and the "pernicious love of fun," and its love of habit and custom confirmed his modest hope of a hardy, lawful, and pragmatic America.

But it was less certain that the unimaginative ministers, mothers, and schoolmasters of Greenfield Hill would care to beget the fearless scientists, the mercantile and artistic titans foreseen in the "fairy hour," that the semi-impoverished farmers would care to toil where "fays delighted dwell," that the creatures of habit would care to overthrow "the power of established custom, and hereditary opinion." Only in the "fairy hour," Dwight soon learned, would footnotes bring forth "poetry."

CHAPTER 3

The Probable America

I The Triumph of Infidelity

INTERNAL DIVISION and continued dependence on Europe were not the only weaknesses Dwight saw in the new republic; he also feared the rise of infidelism. In a sermon preached at Northampton in 1781 Dwight announced that the Revolution marked a turning point for the human race. Coinciding with the climax of the Enlightenment, it placed mankind on the threshold of a universal improvement. He found in the American cause one expression of the progress of knowledge in the century, of the growth of science, the end of superstition, the resultant cosmopolitanism which "effectually extirpates the homebred surliness of solitude"[1] (his notion, apparently, of a cosmopolitan tone). He rejoiced that an independent America offered "a stage of society most friendly to genius," where the mind, contemplating America's novelty and endless opportunity, "is invited, is charmed, to venture far in every path of science and refinement."

Such sentiments were commonplace, but Dwight viewed the moral results of this "great progress of knowledge" as profoundly uncertain. He quoted the scriptural prediction that, on the eve of doomsday, knowledge and science would be thriving. And the surrounding social chaos persuaded him that the present was not the beginning of a new age but the end of the world. The same war that set a stage friendly to human genius had polluted the national character: "This very war, a judgment which ought to awaken repentance and humiliation, hath produced a dissipation of thought, a prostitution of reason, a contempt of religion, a disdain of virtue, a deliberation in vice, and an universal levity and corruption of soul, before unseen and unimagined." What spread this national rot, he believed, was a corrosive spirit of skepticism. He pointed out that skeptics aided progress by attacking bigotry, by questioning civil establishments of religion and the restriction of moral inquiry. But their intention, he warned, was to destroy the kingdom of God. He ended his sermon with a pulpit-thumping call for hard religion, free grace, and a sense of man's dependence, for he was convinced that "progress" had gone too far.

Dwight's remarks at Northampton typify the post-Revolution concern over the low state of American Christianity. David Ramsay also thought the country's military, political, and literary character improved by the war, but its moral character ruined; and Ezra Stiles, foreseeing a struggle between rationalism and revelation, wrote that the clergy would have to defend no particular doctrine but religion itself. The rise of freethought in America was a complex phenomenon. Dwight believed, somewhat narrowly, that infidelity had entered America by contagion during the war; sophisticated foreign troops had contaminated innocent natives. One should add that all American contacts with Europe advanced Deistic thinking in America, since the Puritan theocracy no longer exerted a vital counter force and since the first Great Awakening and the conflicting claims of various Protestant denominations had created a new tolerance of different sects.[2] Even before 1780 a mild form of Deism had spread throughout the colonies.

To alarm New Englanders about creeping skepticism, Dwight wrote *The Triumph of Infidelity,* an ironic narrative in a thousand lines of heroic verse. Both of the slightly differing versions which appeared in 1788 appeared anonymously; and Dwight, who left no manuscript of the poem, never acknowledged it. Noah Webster, seemingly unaware of Dwight's authorship, in a single issue of his magazine reviewed *The Conquest of Canäan* with fervent praise but reviewed *The Triumph of Infidelity* with slashing contempt. No one else, however, doubted that the author was Dwight—nor should any one: the ideas expressed in the poem, and much of the diction and imagery, recur in Dwight's other writings.[3]

For the exaggerated harshness and scurrility of the verse, Dwight drew on Pope through "The Anarchiad," whose success probably inspired Dwight to write the *Triumph.* What Dwight knew of infidel writers seems derived less from Deistic works than from John Leland's *View of the Principal Deistical Writers.* Dwight may also have drawn on Jonathan Edwards' *History of Redemption* (1786), for his account of the major periods of belief and unbelief closely follows Edwards' chronology. But the controlling model for the *Triumph* was the form Dwight had practiced since his tutorship: the rising glory poem. Earlier he had traced the growth of America in terms of evolving and decaying empires; now he traces the growth of infidelity in terms of the rise and fall of Satan's "empire" on earth.

A summary suggests not only the scope of the poem, but also its apparent aimlessness, which has puzzled critics since Dwight's time. The poem falls into two parts of nearly equal length. The first surveys the history of infidelism in ancient and modern times. The second combines a history of infidelity in America with an attack on the Old Light minister Charles Chauncy. In both parts the protagonist is Satan.

Part One opens during the last phase of the Revolution, "ERE yet the Briton left our happy shore." [4] On a cloud, attended by whirlwinds, dragons, and fire, the "prince of darkness" arrives in America, the "realms of freedom, peace, and virtue." Satan remarks the difficulty of winning men to his cause: "From deepest ill what good perpetual springs;/What order shines, where blest confusion lay,/And from the night of death, what splendid day?" (6). When Satan recounts the history of his efforts in terms of the cyclical succession of Christian and infidel nations, Dwight in effect is adapting Edwards' *History of Redemption* to the form of the rising glory poem: paganism; succeeded by apostolic Christianity; succeeded by Goths, Huns, and the papacy; succeeded by Calvin and Luther; succeeded by Charles II.

Nearing the present, Satan tells how such infidel writers as Shaftesbury and Bolingbroke spread doubt by showing that

> No system here, of truth, to man is given;
> There my own doctrines speak the voice of heaven;
> While God, with smiling eyes, alike surveys
> The pagan mysteries, and the christian praise.
> While here on earth no virtuous man was found,
> There saints, like pismires, swarm'd the molehill round;
> Like maggots, crawl'd Caffraria's entrail'd forts;
> Or mushroom'd o'er Europa's putrid courts;
> To deist clubs familiar dar'd retire,
> Or howl'd, and powaw'd, round the Indian fire. . .
>
> (13-14)

Meanwhile, Francis Bacon, Isaac Newton, John Locke, and Bishop

Berkeley try to show the true God. But smaller "fry"—John Toland, Matthew Tindal, Anthony Collins—aided by the "powder'd beaux and boobies" of fashion, win small victories, although few read them. Satan, to bolster his failing troops, rides in a cloud of night to Scotland. There, "in the cobwebs of a college room/ I found my best Amanuensis, Hume." Satan gives Hume sublime, nonsensical dreams, "Pure, genuine dross," and helps spread Hume's confabulations: that no effect has a cause, that Chance rules the universe, that "All beings happen. . . ." Fearing that Hume will prove too dull to read, Satan flies to France and inspires Voltaire, whose superficial wit can prove anything false or true, at whim: "Before his face no Jew could tell what past;/ Or know the right from left, the first from last." Voltaire finds the abode of Truth—a well in China—and taps his Oriental source for notions which, if told to children, would begin "At a time. . . ." Voltaire's Orientalism is presented with special derision:

> Mid idiot Mandarins, and baby Kings,
> And dwarf Philosophers, in leading-strings,
> Mid senseless votaries of less senseless Fo,
> Wretches who nothing even seem'd to know,
> Bonzes, with souls more naked than their skin,
> All brute without, and more than brute within,
> From Europe's rougher sons the goddess shrunk,
> Tripp'd in her iron shoes, and sail'd her junk.
>
> (18-19)

Aided by Hume, Voltaire, Priestley, and assorted Deists and papists, Satan wins numerous victories. To all classes of men he shows vice as benign, and God as imperfect; and he paves the way to sin.

His power ascendant in Europe, Satan has moved to America to continue his work:

> *In this wild waste,* where Albion's lights revive,
> New dangers threaten and new evils live.
> Here a dread race, my sturdiest foes design'd,
> Patient of toil, of firm and vigorous mind,
> Pinion'd with bold research to truth's far coast,
> By storms undaunted, nor in oceans lost,
> With dire invasion, error's realm assail,
> And all my hardy friends before them fail.
>
> (22)

The second half of the poem concerns mainly the Old Light (or more accurately the Universalist) theologian, Charles Chauncy. Chauncy and his followers are Satan's American champions, while his archenemy is the living spirit of Jonathan Edwards. Edwards disclosed in his one lifetime, Satan complains, more of gospel truth than all mankind before him; and he sees that infidelity can combat Edwards' influence only by making virtue seem easy. To thus disarm "conscience of her thorns" and to preach whatever "flatters sinning man," Satan at first employs Ethan Allen, the "great Clodhopping oracle"; but Allen proves ineffectual and unreadable. That is when, vengeful, Satan lights on Chauncy. He persuades the nearly senile minister that "saints the shortest way pursue," and prompts him to write a "mysterious work."

Satan aids Chauncy by supplying him a host of disciples who appear in the poem under as many monograms and pseudonyms, which Dwight's contemporaries deciphered as prominent political personalities. First Satan uses "M*****" who, "scampering from bailiffs," teaches men the "dirtiest ridicule of things most holy,/ And dirtier flattery of sin and folly." "M*****" and Chauncy together produce the doctrine of "Salvation for all men." They hold that "God must help the perjur'd, as the true," and that all sins will be forgiven. Other politicians arise to contest with Chauncy for the honor of being Satan's minion. "Florio" claims to beat Chauncy even in pride: "Two whores already in my chariot ride." Another grabs his bags of gold, boasts he no longer will help widows and orphans, and teaches that "pious usury now's the road to heaven."

On a large plain now appears a Dwightean "numerous train" wishing to gain from Chauncy and his crew the confidence to sin: a "half putrid Epicure," his "lips with turtle green"; a lecher, a "high-fed horse, for others wives who neigh'd"; "Hypocrisy, in sober brown." Among them is "the smooth Divine." Dwight's portrait of this ultimate Chauncyite achieved a popularity independent of the poem and was several times reprinted. The "smooth Divine" will not scare sinners by hard religion; instead, he issues "Trite, fireside, moral seasaws." He laughs at rich men's jokes, praises their wives' dresses, dines on pampered turkies, and on his parish rounds,

> Smoak'd with each goody, thought her cheese excell'd;
> Her pipe he lighted, and her baby held.

Or plac'd in some great town, with lacquer'd shoes,
Trim wig, and trimmer gown, and glistening hose,
He bow'd, talk'd politics, learn'd manners mild.

(31)

Finally a squabbling parliament of Chauncyites arrives: the unprincipled man, neither Deist nor Christian, to whom good and evil are the same, "Jehovah, Jove, the Lama, or the Devil;/ Mohammed's braying, or Isaiah's lays"; "Demas," a sober Christian until he traveled to Europe, now a theater-goer and wig-wearer: "Shall powder'd heads . . . be sent to hell?"; and "Euclio," driven by passions and appetites, a sinner despite his conscience.

Satan rushes forth among the host in his chariot while "expressive emblems," such as Old Age and Vanity, swell the scene. Amidst the tumult Chauncy himself appears and shouts out his doctrine: "Hell is no more, or no more to be fear'd." The ecstatic throng applauds. But, momentarily, conscience strikes; guilt and remorse trouble the "dreadful train." Instantly, however, "sophistic wishes" blunt their pangs: the flames of hell recede; sin seems less dangerous; God less fearful. And, no longer unmanned by guilt, more boldly than ever Chauncy's host, and even decent Christians, lie, cheat, turn coat, swear, defame, and whore. Truth and Virtue, aghast at the new sources of falsehood opened to mankind, sigh. Satan eyes the scene, and in the concluding lines of the poem,

. . . proud with triumph and now vex'd with spleen,
Mark'd all the throng, beheld them all his own,
And to his cause no friend of virtue won:
Surpriz'd, enrag'd, he wing'd his sooty flight,
And hid beneath the pall of endless night.

(40)

Readers since Dwight's time have been puzzled by the very subject of the poem. In the concluding lines, for instance, Satan "beheld them all his own" (even decent Christians), yet "to his cause no friend of virtue won." He is "proud with triumph" yet "vex'd with spleen"; he flees "Supriz'd, enrag'd," although the poem describes his unobstructed triumph.[5] Does the poem attack skeptics, or unorthodox fellow Calvinists? Did Dwight, as one critic suggests, intend to satirize Deism and materialism, but turn to heterodox Calvinists for lack of better material? Did he, as another suggests, intend simply an attack on the liberal Old Light theology and the consequences of its wide acceptance in New England?

Actually, the poem attacks not only skeptics or liberal Calvinists, but all the forces of social instability. Its subject is political. In the poem Dwight specifies that Christianity and political order have the same basis; to mock God is to mock all governance: "The same principles, which support or destroy christianity, alike support or destroy political order and government." Dwight knew the distinction between Deists and unorthodox Calvinists; but he saw no difference between Deists and democrats. The two parts of the poem form a single attack against whatever ideas, sects, and personalities Dwight considered friendly to democracy and unfriendly to social order. "Infidelity" became for him a catch-all abomination. Toward the end of his life, it meant anyone and anything he loathed for any reason. This underlying quarrel with democracy fails to emerge, partly because of Dwight's habitual failure to maintain a point of view. In the *Conquest,* he ineptly attributed the character of Milton's Satan to Joshua; in the *Triumph,* he makes Satan praise Edwards and laud "faith's etherial shield." With the entry of the "numerous train" of lechers and epicures, he unexpectedly shifts the point of view away from Satan; with the introduction of "Euclio," another new narrator appears who laments Euclio's fortune and mourns those "charm'd to madness by the old serpent's breath." In the parliament of Chauncyites, as among the Israelites, it is impossible to tell whether Satan, or Chauncy, or some other narrator is speaking.

These technical ineptitudes confuse Dwight's argument. He expressed his contempt for democracy more clearly in "an address to the ministers of the gospel," which he published the same year as the *Triumph.* Here, against the background of Shays's Rebellion, he enumerated the causes of social unrest: too frequent elections (which tempt to drunkenness), too many lawsuits (breeding discord among neighbors), the election of magistrates and militia officers by the people, the admission of boys and girls as servants into genteel families, and a free press.[6] What his "address" blames on democratic practices, the *Triumph* blames on infidelism. Dwight's assault on Chauncy, although posed in doctrinal terms, is purely an assault on democracy, for Dwight felt that to impugn hard religion was to undermine the state by removing powerful "motives" for decorous behavior. The internecine wars of New England Congregationalism, whether or not fought over the half-way covenant or Arminianism, had always at stake, ultimately, the nature of New England society. Chauncy's doctrine of universal salvation threatened the order of New England by eliminating an important reason for acting well—the fear of eternal punishment.

As minister of the First Church of Boston, Chauncy preached an optimistic, merchant-class gospel. He argued an infinitely benevolent God whose main concern was man's happiness. Privately and thoughtfully, he developed the notion that the eternal damnation of sinners was inconsistent with God's plan, which aimed at the happiness of the system as a whole, including businessmen. In 1784 he published anonymously *The Salvation of All Men: The Grand Thing Aimed at in the Scheme of God,* and it opens: "The whole human race are considered in the following work as made for happiness." This conclusion, we will see, the benevolent atmosphere of the second Great Awakening forced Dwight himself to accept. In his later *Theology,* he admitted that the biblical concept of eternal punishment was perplexing. It turned, he argued, on the interpretation of the scriptural image of consuming fire and on the meaning of "forever." Having by this time abandoned his own orthodoxy, he decided that the fires were figurative and that man cannot understand the concept of infinity; therefore he left the question open.

In the *Triumph,* however, Dwight makes Chauncy parody his doctrine by preaching that "hell is but a school for sin": "Then would you lay your own, or others fears,/ Search your own bosoms, or appeal to theirs./Know, what those bosoms wish Heaven must reveal;/And sure no bosom ever wish'd a hell" (37). God tries to make man religious on earth; if that does not work, Chauncy explains, He sends him to hell; if he repents there he is saved; if not, God sends him lower down in hell, "Till with such sinking tir'd, he longs to rise," and is sent straight to heaven.

Many of Dwight's colleagues publicly and strenuously opposed Chauncy's doctrines. Chauncy's most impressive antagonist had been, of course, Jonathan Edwards. In a sense Dwight was continuing the argument his grandfather had lost to Chauncy at Northampton in 1750 when he was removed from his pulpit. But Dwight continued it on new grounds, representing a growing change in the character of the Congregational leadership. Dwight emphasizes in the poem not individual regeneration, as Edwards had, but social order. He ridicules Chauncy because, by promising salvation to gamblers, perjurers, and bad husbands, his doctrines foster social disorder. The key issue for the older conservative Calvinists had always been piety, the dead individual heart; for Dwight, it was becoming *pietas,* social consciousness. Indeed, Edwards welcomed the socially disruptive "enthusiasm" of the first Great Awakening, while Chauncy deplored it, and in this attitude Dwight stood closer to Chauncy than to his grandfather. Unlike Edwards, Dwight feared unleashing passions, even religious passions. He indicts "Euclio," "Florio," and the other sinners not for dooming their souls but for disturbing the peace.

That explains why it is in social terms that Satan always imagines the consequences of Chauncy's doctrines. They create the miser who will "let widows weep," the ingrate who "sold his friend, and country, for a song." During the presidential campaign of 1800, one reviewer identified the pseudonymous characters of the *Triumph* as specific political enemies of Dwight. In the miser, he saw Jeremiah Wadsworth, a chief stockholder in the Bank of North America, which at one time charged interest of ninety-six percent a year (Dwight was a director of the rival Eagle Bank). He identified the "smooth Divine" as James Dana of the Yale corporation, with which Dwight had bickered since his student days. He identified Satan's whoremongering minion "Florio" as Charles Cotesworth Pinckney. Whether or not Dwight had specific personalities in mind, his animus was clearly social and political, not doctrinal.

The political basis of the poem explains why Dwight allied the New England Calvinist Chauncy with the French infidel Voltaire; and the discrepancy between their statures is one of the poem's calculated effects. Dwight links Chauncy with Voltaire, Hume, and Shaftesbury to show how toxic Chauncy's doctrines are; but he also shows that no American, certainly no New Englander, could be so poisonous as a European, much less a Frenchman. His narrative of the rise of infidelity in Europe and America contains also a "glorious contrast" between Europe and America. He shows America endangered not by Infidelity but, as it were, infidelity. The first line of the poem—"ERE yet the Briton left our happy shore"—expresses a nationalistic bias which subtly rules the whole. After leaving Europe in triumph, Satan journeys to what he calls the "realms of freedom, peace, and virtue." He prophesies the success of his doctrines, although "yon haughty world their worth deny" and although in America dwell his "sturdiest foes."

Dwight's splenetic attack on Chauncyism in America is balanced by his claim that Americans resist the virulent, European strains of Infidelity. Satan bemoans his disciples' failure in America: "Their toils, their efforts, and their arts are vain." Much of the ambiguity of the *Triumph* results from Dwight's new version of the "glorious contrast." Earlier he wrote quite simply as the friend of America and the critic of Europe. Shocked by the lawlessness in the nation, he now found himself the critic of Europe and America both. He did not yet doubt, however, that America could be redeemed; he wished to criticize it for slipping toward anarchy and at the same time to defend it in contrast to "Europa's putrid courts."

For this reason, Dwight tempered the otherwise satanic picture of Chauncy. In contrast to the willfully vicious Voltaire, Chauncy is "led astray" by Satan, who takes advantage of his years: "Now palsied age has dimm'd his mental sight,/I'll rouse the sage his master's laws to fight" (25). A number of times Dwight commends Chauncy's good works, while Satan undertakes to "wipe from heaven's fair book his faith and prayer." Unlike a European infidel, Chauncy has no desire to "charge the sacred books with lies." Aging, he merely mistakes the Bible's promise of eternal punishment for a "harmless trifling with the human kind." He considers the idea of damnation a fatherly ploy designed to "curb the rebel, man." Dwight presents Chauncy's doctrine of universal salvation as a blunder, not a blasphemy, and Chauncy himself not as an enemy but as a "false friend."

In Dwight's prefatory epistle to Voltaire, he notes that "ingenious interpretation" of the Bible is a more effective "annoyance" than ridicule of it. By misrepresentation, "the secret and deadly dirk is plunged to the heart of unsuspecting friendship, unhappily trusting the smooth-faced assassin." Later, Satan cunningly decides to use Chauncy to produce a "cheated gospel," which will do most harm by creating most trust. Like Dwight, Satan reasons that "False friends may stab, when foes must fly the field." By recovering the image of the "stabbing friend" from his preface, Dwight implicates Chauncy not in outright ridicule and slander, the European vices, but in misrepresentation caused by his advanced age and weak eyes. Even then his sin is not willful misrepresentation but oversubtlety. Chauncy has read the Bible too closely, "read in Greek," and discovered that "the page reveal'd our cause sustains,/ When search'd with cunning, and when gloss'd with pains" (36).[7] Dwight does not condone Chauncy, however, for his innocence; indeed, his good intentions make his doctrines pernicious. Decent but humble Christians, who also take the Bible seriously, trustingly accept the erudite Chauncy's version of what it says.

In this way Dwight both allies Chauncy and Voltaire, and distinguishes them. Chauncy unwillingly misrepresents the Bible and makes religion easy; Voltaire treacherously misrepresents it and makes religion ridiculous. Placed beside Voltaire, Chauncy seems dangerous but not malicious—a relative infidel. While attacking Chauncy, Dwight would not afford already critical Europeans the spectacle of a degenerate America. His double attitude toward Chauncy creates the seeming contradictions of the last lines of the poem. Satan is "Now proud with triumph, and now vex'd with spleen" because Chauncyism gives him only a partial victory. It teaches men the wrong way to heaven, but teaches a way. Satan wins no "friends of virtue" because he is in America.

To establish a double viewpoint, protecting Chauncy while belittling him, Dwight again made extensive use of footnotes. The unsigned notes to the poem represent Dwight speaking in his own voice, but those signed by "Anon." and "Scriblerus" represent Satan's infidel friends. (Dwight makes a character out of "Anon.," spoofing the anonymous publications of the Deists.) Satan considers the infidels his dupes, mere instruments for building his empire; and they prove "false friends" of infidelity. By dramatic irony "Anon." and "Scriblerus" disclose their own stupidity; and, through it, the stupidity of Satan's cause. The unsavory infidels expand "plantain" as a plant which "when swallowed by Voltaire . . . will help to expel gripes of conscience, as a decoction of Ginseng will those of the flatulent cholic, full as well as warm water." They annotate Newton and Locke as the "names of a few silly men, whose minds were too small to comprehend the nature and evidences of Infidelity."

In one instance Dwight wittily causes "Scriblerus" to reveal the befuddlement of Satan himself. When Satan claims to have flown to Scotland to see Hume and then to France to visit Voltaire,

Your gallant deeds, in Greece, or haughty Rome,
By Maro sung, or Homer's harp sublime,
Had charm'd the world's wide round. . . .

(IV, 392-96)

Dwight used "yonder starry home," the past, much as he used the millennium and God—to overcome his conflicts by obliterating moral difficulties. As a poet, he had no power to express a single, however divided, state of mind. Warring ideas, opposed feelings, appear in contrasting parts of the poem, isolated from each other. Dwight never digests them into single but complex images. In Joel Barlow's sense, Dwight was often speaking a foreign language, voicing ideals that must to himself have seemed unreal.

Property and "Competence" alone do not create and keep the happiness of Connecticut; for in Dwight's view, they are aided by appropriate religious and secular education. The dying minister of Part Five urges for his parishioners common religious practices designed to maintain social decorum: Bible reading, regular church attendance, prayer, religious instruction for children, charity to the sick and the poor, and hard work. The demands of secular education Dwight treats more expansively. In 1779, while in Northampton, he had begun, as noted earlier, a coeducational academy with a curriculum similar to Yale's. Its success was such that Ezra Stiles feared Dwight's academy as a rival to Yale;[10] indeed, a few Yale students asked his leave to study with Dwight. In 1783, Dwight decided to continue the school at Greenfield Hill. At its peak it enrolled fifty or sixty students, including some from the middle states (the prominent New York Livingstons sent their sons), from the South, from France, and from the West Indies. Dwight loved teaching because it allowed him to inculcate the good habits and natural virtue he thought compatible with republican government.

In *Greenfield Hill* Dwight opposed his own teaching experience to modern theories of education. Such theories, he notes, like political theories, are "published by men, of genius indeed, but wholly inexperienced in education; men who educate children on paper, as a geometrician circumnavigates the globe, in half a dozen spherical triangles." Part Six, "The Farmer's Advice to the Villagers," describes secular education and child-rearing in an ideal republic. The farmer-narrator's common sense and simplicity make him the standard of earthly good. He is Dwight's sage, an

"Scriblerus" notes that "Satan seems guilty of an anachronism here, Voltaire being the eldest writer of the two." This footnote may seem only an afterthought designed to justify a real anachronism in the poem; but Dwight had used the same device in *The Conquest of Canäan,* where an elderly beggar approaches Irad saying, upon "thy head have twice ten summers run." Irad is eighteen, not twenty. Hoping to dramatize the old man's infirmity, Dwight notes clumsily below: "This is a mistake of the sage."

Other footnotes in the *Triumph* allow the infidel annotators to expose each other, as they argue nonsensically under a *blague* of learned discourse: "Anon." expands "Clodhopping" as the "new name elegantly given to man" in Allen's *Oracles of Reason*; directly below, "Scriblerus" points out that "the annotator above mistakes, in calling this epithet a new name. I could easily shew, by a series of learned deductions, that Clodhopper was the very original name of mankind, when they wore tails." Pointedly, Dwight gave three-fourths of the annotation to the part of the poem dealing with Voltaire, again stressing the Frenchman's difference from Chauncy.

The ambiguous effect of the *Triumph* is rooted in Dwight's wish to attack Chauncy while maintaining the "glorious contrast" between Europe and America. The image of the "false friend" intimates Dwight's response to the social dislocations and political intrigues of the 1780's and 1790's. He had begun to take a conspiratorial view of history. The *Triumph* speaks of "Infidels injured unwittingly by their friends," of the "friends of freedom," of Satan's "open friends," "hardy friends," "false friends," and, of course, the "friend of virtue" Satan cannot win. The poem abounds in imagery of concealment, disfiguration, and imposture: cloaks, webs, palls, the Hypocrite in brown, the smooth Divine, the medieval doctors who "Maz'd the dim soul," Charles II's "webs of sophism," Hume's "maim'd image" of God, and so on. "False friend" resonates with the suspicions of a revolutionary generation uncertain of its allies and with Dwight's new awareness of French perfidy.

"False friend" is also symptomatic of Dwight's increasing disenchantment with America and of the distress that accompanied it. It echoes afar the chagrin that drove him to write anonymous, ambiguous attacks against his own colleagues. His old metaphor of the rise and fall of empires, the eternal warfare between good and evil, Americans and Europeans, Federalists and Jeffersonians, and Old and New Lights did not suit his subtle position. He admired much in England, he still shared with Jefferson a belief in America and with Chauncy a desire to widen the church. For his tirade against a mixed bag of backsliders, allegorical figures, disguised or unnamed contemporaries, Europeanized Americans, he supplied a single tone and a single doctrinal idiom. He failed to make clear that behind his hatred of Chauncy, Origen, and Jeremiah Wadsworth was a love not of correct doctrine but of the peace and quiet of Greenfield Hill.

Upon its publication, the *Triumph* was roasted and misunderstood. In July, 1788, Noah Webster summarized the poem in the *American Magazine* and called it a "jumble of unmeaning epithets, or an unnatural association of ideas." [8] He found the versification harsh, the wit forced, the ideas obscure, the theology puerile. Particularly, he disliked the abusive treatment of the Chinese religion, the imperious tone, and the generally unchristian and unrefined manner. He noted that anyone who could lump together Shaftesbury and Priestley with Chauncy and Allen "can hardly be a candidate for that heaven of love and benevolence which the Scripture informs us is prepared for good men." Webster failed to see that the ideas are all naturally associated with social harmony, that Dwight offers no theology, that he emphatically distinguishes between the American Chauncy and the English Priestley, and that the abusive passages are spoken by Satan or his henchmen. (His caustic review marked the end of Dwight's association with him, although Webster was almost certainly unaware of Dwight's authorship.) Despite Dwight's anonymity, the poem was immediately attributed to him. In his diary, Ezra Stiles recorded reading "*Dr* Dwights Triumph of Infidelity"; and, while admiring its "beautiful Satyre," he complained that Dwight should have confined himself to Deists, and not shown "a number of protestant erroneous Divines"[9] as subserving their cause. The trouncing of Chauncy distressed Stiles, who protested that Chauncy was not a Deist, a charge Dwight never raised against him. Like Webster, Stiles regretted Dwight's (really Satan's) slander of the Chinese and Dwight's (really Satan's) tone, the "ill nature, Acrimony & Malevolence," by which Dwight "overshot the Mark, & hurt the Cause which he meant to defend."

Stiles saw, accurately, that Dwight's intention backfired; but the poem is not simply an attack on Deism nor is every voice in the poem Dwight's. Stiles's opinion of Dwight, moreover, always took heat from his suspicion that Dwight craved his job. The abrasive tone of the *Triumph* disturbed English reviewers as well. One confessed himself shocked that "the malignant spirit, which is breathed out in these lines against all who do not bear the badge of orthodoxy; should have resided in the bosom of an eminent Christian divine."[10] The reviewer seems to have known that Dwight wrote the poem; but, ironically, he seems not to have known who "Dwight" was: *"Timothy Dwight, D.D., &c,* sounds very like fiction. We hope this may be the case."

II *The Conquest of Infidelity*

Dwight followed up his oblique, anonymous attack on the causes of social unrest with a series of public attacks. He began wielding the influence of his pulpit and name to reverse the tide of infidelity. He became ever more critical of America; and, as he addressed more urgent and specific issues, he turned increasingly from "poetry" to prose. As his vision of national possibilities shrank, so did the gap between the minister and the patriot. For, to combat rising democracy, Dwight used his Calvinist training in the service of his Federalist politics. He began urging a return to something like theocratic government.

Dwight looked unhappily at the Constitution and the new Bill of Rights as purely secular instruments which failed to provide strong "motives." At the opening of the 1791 session of the legislature, he delivered a lengthy sermon entitled "Virtuous Rulers a National Blessing." Such election sermons had been the custom of the New England states since the seventeenth century. And like a seventeenth-century Puritan, Dwight imagined the relation between the state and its citizens not in terms of a Bill of Rights but in terms of the Mosaic code. By a state law of 1791, a non-Congregationalist had only to certify that he regularly attended his own church to avoid paying dues to the Congregationalist Church. The law released many from the moral and political sway of the clergy. To counter this local loss of Congregational power, Dwight sought a national executive modeled on such Puritan worthies as John Winthrop. He called for no mere politician, but for a man who rigorously embodied the good he sought to do.

Amid many parallels between the situation of the ancient Hebrews and the contemporary Americans, Dwight argued that the proper motive for a ruler is not conscience or honor but righteousness. The leader's first duty is support of religion. Without pleading openly for a state church, Dwight demanded a theocratic leader who would advance the general cause of religion "by steadfastly opposing immorality, by employing and honouring the just, by contemning the vicious."[11] His own virtuous conduct would make the ruler a sort of God on earth, acting the character which is "the nearest resemblance" to God's by extending His kingdom of righteousness. Dwight only hoped that such a political redeemer would arise. He feared that the spirit of the times favored lukewarm leaders and timid administrations, "the midway inoffensive course of magistracy." A bold course of action would provoke conspiratorial opposition, and would lose votes. To rouse the fainthearted Dwight recalled, as New Englanders had been recalling since the time of Wigglesworth, the "moral glory" of the forefathers. Such a reminder asked for toughened moral fiber as well as an actual return to Puritan forms of government, or at least to the Puritan leadership. In effect, Dwight now required that the federal government personified in a "Virtuous Ruler" do what the Connecticut clergy no longer was empowered to do.

Dwight renewed his quarrel with the Constitution in a discourse concerning "The True Means of Establishing Public Happiness" (1795). Against the background of the Whisky Rebellion, a proof of the Constitution's failure, he argued that freedom is not enough: men can be free and miserable. The aim of life, rather, is happiness, which depends on virtue, which depends on "Religious Education and Public Worship," which the Constitution ignored.[12] Dwight criticized the ideals and institutions of the existing government, although a decade before he had warmly endorsed them. He no longer regarded the vast size of America as a blessing; it made government too complicated, too wealthy, and too showy. He believed the government should not expand, but concentrate on forming good personal character and self-governance in its citizens, a sense of propriety, a realistic vision of "such liberty, as is suited to the condition of man."

Such knowledge could be conferred only by experience or revelation; theories of liberty "ought to be placed on the same level with the professed fictions of poets, and to be written in verse, and not in sober prose." As in *Greenfield Hill,* Dwight implied that, since the government of Connecticut offered a tested way of producing happiness, America ought to be Connecticutized. His enumeration of the specific kinds of social knowledge citizens ought to have recalls the collective wisdom of his pastoral narrators: knowledge of the means of promoting the common interest, of the beneficent influence of peace, the desirable character of political candidates, the importance of domestic education, the advantages of mild conduct, the profit of virtue.

The gist of Dwight's "Discourse" is its bid for an increased role of Connecticut in the government, and of the ministry in Connecticut. Dwight had afforded the shortest part of *Greenfield Hill* to the counsel of the dying minister; now he saw the ministry as the key to implementing social happiness. Only the ministry, by making virtue popular, could ensure social order: "intimate and inseparable is the permanent and sufficient support of the ministers of religion with virtue, and of course with the existence, and the stability, of public happiness." Forswearing his ideal of "Sweet harmless elves" in "Freedom's household," he advised new, stringent applications of religious discipline. Parents should give their children religious instruction at home, schoolmasters at school; the morals of all teachers should be scrutinized by a morals commission.

In the same year, the death of Ezra Stiles offered Dwight a new command-post for his war on infidelity: the Yale presidency. At first Dwight refused the position because his parish at Greenfield Hill, which theoretically had appointed him for life, voted its unwillingness to release him. But the matter went before the county organ or "consociation" which, with Dwight's consent, voted his dismission. Despite his initial rejection of the post, Dwight had eyed the presidency for a long time. With great zeal he began administering a small-town college (New Haven was not much larger than Fairfield) with one hundred and ten students; in the course of an extremely distinguished presidency, he built it into a national institution. He added professors of law, languages, ecclesiastical history, and chemistry (Benjamin Silliman, whose lectures Dwight himself attended); he set up laboratories, a botanical garden, and a medical school, and he carried much of the teaching load himself. He became professor of divinity in addition to president, turning back more than half of his two salaries into expanding the college. He renewed his duties as senior tutor by instructing the seniors in belles lettres and oratory. His appointments stood until the middle of the nineteenth century; for fifty years, Yale-trained ministers and teachers migrated across the country, spreading his teachings.

Dwight offered students a practical but scholarly education under a faculty united in political and religious beliefs. Those beliefs were, one student wrote, "very nearly the same with those of Calvin and Washington." Dwight set his two idols the task of restoring order at Yale itself. The nationwide lawlessness and turmoil he lamented had become a collegiate fad. A Dartmouth student found only one professing Christian in the class of 1799; at Princeton, only tutors and three or four students attended prayer-meetings; Yale, whose college church numbered two members, was in an ungodly state itself, Dwight felt, with flagrant disorder, impiety, and wickedness. Fashionable students ridiculed divine revelation, denounced organized religion, adored Tom Paine, and named themselves "D'Alembert" and "Diderot."

Dwight fought back at once. In his first baccalaureate sermon as president he warned: "You will find all men substantially alike, and all naturally ignorant and wicked. You will find every man pleased, not merely to be free, but to tyrannize; and to indulge without restraint, and without degree, both appetite and passion; and to be impatient of every law, which in any degree restrains either."[13] Twenty years before, in his valedictory address at Yale in 1776, he had jubilantly declared that mankind had "learned to despise the shackles of custom, and the chains of authority." Now his single hope was that students return home with an unshakable, traditional faith. Like Ezra Stiles before him, he proposed open debates on religion. Taking on all comers, he tried to expose the irrelevancies and illogic of infidel arguments. He delivered a special course of lectures on the evidences of divine revelation. He fired instructors suspected of infidel leanings. Ceremoniously, he took down portraits of Joel Barlow.

Dwight delivered his most impassioned assault on his students' views to the graduating class of 1797: "The Nature, and Danger, of Infidel Philosophy." The discourse moves from sweetly logical, formal refutations of infidel philosophy to eruptions of acid invective that reveal Dwight's authoritarian temper. Here his enemy was not the legion of minor social ills loosely represented by the enfeebled Chauncy, or the barely tangible results of a too-secular Constitution; it was the intoxicated clamor for Liberty ending in the tumbrils and guillotines of the French Revolution. Even in the dozens of logical examples meant to disclose inconsistencies in the thought of Hobbes, Shaftesbury, and Hume, Dwight's hated white whale is clearly no single doctrine but all abstract thought, all philosophy, all intellect which presumes to upset the status quo.

With smug approval Dwight quotes Plutarch to show that Socrates and Plato were "as incontinent and intemperate as any slave," that Aristotle was a "fop, a debaucher, and a traitor."[14] He claims that, like his pagan precursors, Hume died "playing at whist, reading Lucian's dialogues, and making silly attempts at wit." Reading Paine and toying with Liberty, Dwight warned his students, begets "falshood [*sic*], perjury, fraud, theft, piracy, robbery, oppression, revenge, fornication, and adultery."

In its appeal to the young and the ignorant, Dwight believed, lay the special danger of infidel philosophy. Like many other Federalists, he feared the spread of Deism to the combustible lower classes. He explained to his students that, beside the dazzling ingenuity of infidel arguments, Scripture is vulnerable since its statements, while factual, pertain to remote events incapable of certain proof. Having spent his own youth as the spokesman for fashionable ideals, he particularly feared that his students would own infidel ideas merely to be stylish. He explained how infidels snare the innocent: they pretend that the learned share their opinions; they assert (as a younger Dwight had asserted) that, before them, mankind groveled in ignorant bondage to authority. Also, fashionable young men might be unwilling to announce themselves as Christians, first because a general bias against Christianity exists, due to the breakdown of moral restraint, and because infidelity offers license, while Christianity is "a system of restraint on every passion and every appetite."

Dwight's hostility to Europe and to the excesses of Liberty had begun shortly after Independence. Events in France intensified and embittered it. As the French Revolution gave the country a sense of party demarcation, it gave Dwight's conservatism a specific thrust. It clarified his discontent with the emerging character of America. It freed him from "gay prospects" and from makeshifts like "Competence." Flattering estimates of America's future, the equal division of its land, the defense of its Chauncys would not, he decided, make America work. To succeed, the new country needed deliberate disengagement from Europe, immediate restoration of clerical authority, and a crackdown on heresies.

Two events now confirmed Dwight's views: the "XYZ" affair, which further proved French perfidy, and the revelation of a supposed plot by the "Illuminati" to overthrow the government. While John Adams' publication of the "XYZ" correspondence aroused anti-French sentiment and cast disrepute on Enlightenment rationalism, it also drew public attention to Dwight. His warnings against Chauncyism, soft religion, and "false friends" had been right; and he emerged as a political prophet. The second event, which brought many conservative New Englanders to the brink of hysteria, was the exposure of a German rationalist sect, the "Illuminati," which, its detractors claimed, had formed branches in the United States to abolish Christianity and overturn civil government.

In John Robison's *Proofs of a Conspiracy against all the Religions and Governments of Europe Carried on in Secret Meetings of Free Masons, Illuminati, and Reading Societies,* appalled New Englanders learned how Illuminists had gathered disbanded Jesuits, atheists, Republicans, free lovers, and communists into one messianic conspiracy under the leadership of Voltaire, Diderot, Rousseau, and Condorcet—all for the sake, Dwight wrote, of destroying "civil and domestic government, the right of property, marriage, natural affection, chastity, and decency . . . under the pretence of enlarged Philanthropy and of giving mankind liberty and equality."[15]

Dwight's tone of awe-struck revelation, of things suddenly making sense, shows how New England greeted the disclosure of the Illuminist plot. Dwight made it his function to dissociate the idea of Liberty from everything French. He prepared a sermon for the Fourth of July, 1798, "The Duty of Americans, at the Present Crisis." Insensitive to his language as usual, he borrowed Tom Paine's word; but his message was violently anti-libertarian. From his pulpit he lay bare the plot: a "secret academy" composed of men of "ardour" existed, where books were being "formed, altered, forged imputed as posthumous to deceased writers of reputation" and published "at the lowest price" and circulated "through all classes of men."[16] This society came to America in 1786 (during

Shays's Rebellion), where it has since been undermining society, property, and chastity; waging "an open and professed war against God"; and encouraging "faction, rebellion, the ruin of peace, and the loss of property." America could be saved by reaffirming its piety, which to Dwight meant returning political power to the Federalist-Congregationalist clergy: "without religion we may possibly retain the freedom of savages, bears and wolves; but not the freedom of New-England."

Dwight proposed an entire separation (short of commercial ties) from that France which breeds harlotry, corruption, and frenzy. He ordered a second Declaration of Independence: "Would you wholly escape, you must be wholly separated. I do not recommend that you must not buy or sell, or exhibit the common offices of justice and good will; but you are bound by the voice of reason, of duty, of safety, and of God, to shun all such connection with them, as will interweave your sentiments or your friendship, your religion or your policy, with theirs." For himself, he would forbid his children infidel works and would rather, he said, they die than become "victims of philosophism."

The "crisis" plummeted Dwight into the dark side of his manicheanism, toward which he had long tended. It gave the upper voice to the Puritan accent that for twenty years had insinuated itself into his high hopes. He begged his audience to trust the God who led the Israelites to Canaan; who would help America to beat France in a war, if necessary; who was preparing the millennium described in the fifth vial of the Book of Revelation; and who, shorn of rhapsody and augury, would let the Connecticut clergy seize power.

Dwight had in mind not only France, of course, but local Jacobins as well. His sermon, delivered amidst fierce factional and party feeling in the country, enraged Connecticut democrats, who angrily denounced Yale. The leader of the opposition, James Cousins Ogden, an Episcopal clergyman in New Hampshire, charged Dwight himself with Illuminism! (In national politics the term had also begun to lose its significance; both parties accused each other of Illuminism.) He blamed Dwight for describing the Christian religion as full of unintelligible mysteries and dubbed him "The head of the Illuminati," ready to propagate "the faith of his grandfather by the power of the sword." Under Dwight's tutelage, Ogden said, Calvinist clubs held secret political meetings; Connecticut had become "almost totally an ecclesiastical state, ruled by the President of the College, as a Monarch."[17] He charged Dwight with controlling religious opinion and politics not only in Connecticut but throughout the United States.

The extent of Dwight's political involvement at this time is unclear; few records of his direct political dealings remain. In the decade before 1800 Connecticut had had hardly any political life in the modern sense. Only after the Republicans formally organized an anticlerical platform for the Jefferson campaign were Federalists forced to bring out their full voting strength and to operate as a party. Whether because of Dwight's influence or not, the Congregational clergy had by the Adams administration become solidly Federalist, and exerted great political power through its parishes and schools. It examined teachers for fitness, conducted prayers at freemen's meetings, helped take the vote, and with the ruling class demanded strong, stable central government. To perpetuate its social prestige and long tenure, the clergy openly preached politics from the pulpit; and, for the sake of conscience and self-preservation, it wished to defeat Jefferson.

Dwight, deservedly or not, became identified as the leader of the Congregational-Federalist interests. He was christened "The Pope of Federalism," "Old Pope Dwight," "The Metropolitan See of Federalism," "His Holiness Pope Timothy" (his brother sometimes appeared in print as "Cardinal Theodore"). As his literary reputation became suddenly magnified, even his belletristic writings came to be seen as expressions of his politics. Ogden denounced how through "poetry, satirical writing, The Triumph of Infidelity," Dwight had put Connecticut "more completely under the administration of a Pope than Italy," and had circulated his "prejudices" through "young men and divines taught by him."[18] After asking Dwight to revise Barlow's edition of Watts's *Psalms,* the General Association of Connecticut refused to publish the verses because of the political bias they detected in Dwight's revisions; nothing in Dwight's version, actually, suggests any political view. The Association published the psalms after Dwight proposed giving a portion of the profits to the Missionary Society. Even then, a reviewer in the *American Mercury* regretted that many clergymen now advised their congregations to use Dwight, solely because anyone using Barlow would be thought "impious and profane," while Dwight was "uncontaminated with any allusions to a republican form of government."[19]

When Dwight's earlier work was exhumed, sinister tendencies were discovered. *The Triumph of Infidelity,* twelve years after its publication, came in for new aspersions. During the election of 1800, Dwight actively supported Charles Cotesworth Pinckney for the vice-presidency; and a new generation of Republican reviewers found delightedly that Dwight had blasted Pinckney as a Deist and infidel in the *Triumph.* A series of articles in the Hartford *American Mercury* named Dwight as the author of the poem and showed the public how, flighty as an infidel, Dwight had reversed his stand:

> A Minister of the Gospel, who ought to be an example to all men, sets at his desk in 1788, hates Yale College, hates Doctors Dana and Chauncy—is in contest with most of his brethren—hates sin and Pinckney, and a thousand more conscious men, puts it all into rhyme—issues it without his name—attacks without mercy men, who had been gaining fair characters before he was born. In 1800 is a President of a College, ay the head of a corporation of which his *milky Preacher* in the above poem is a member—is in high favor with the Clergy, and begins to rebuild the waste of character made by his indignant pen—and first foremost hails his former *hackney coachman of whores* [i.e., Pinckney] as a pious man and real christian.[20]

Dwight was not above the duplicity that the reviewer implied. There was a growing split between Dwight's public and private opinions. As he thundered decency and righteousness from his pulpit, he railed spitefully against a growing number of petty foes in unsigned invectives. The same year that he published his anonymous attack on Chauncy, we have seen, he published a signed "address to the Ministers of the Gospel" pleading for "Christians of different denominations to love each other."[21] He increasingly resorted to anonymous publications to express opinions that he could not express as a cleric and college president.

But no one could confidently identify the unnamed contemporaries and vague doctrinal heresies of the *Triumph* with living contemporaries. In fact, Pinckney's "whoring" did not become a public issue until after the "XYZ" affair and after Hamilton's "Report on the Public Credit," which gave rise to the financial speculation Dwight purportedly reviled, appeared in 1790, two years after the *Triumph* was published. The reviewer's wish to to see Pinckney or Dana in the poem was simply intended to embarrass Dwight. In response, Dwight sent the *Mercury* letters and affidavits proving Pinckney blameless, although without acknowledging his own authorship of the poem.[22]

III The New-England Palladium

But Dwight's troubles were only beginning. Ahead loomed the Napoleonic campaigns, in which he saw confirmed the ruin of Europe and, quite incredibly to him, the defeat of Federalism at the polls in 1800 with the election of Jefferson—Jacobinism fleshed. Meanwhile, resentment against "Pope Dwight" forced him to work underground to protect his own reputation and that of the college. His preaching, like that of many other conservative ministers after the election, became less openly political. He managed, however, to publicize and enforce his anti-democratic views through collaboration with Episcopalians, through his influence on friends in the ruling circle of Connecticut politics, through classroom colloquies which he used for political indoctrination, and through pseudonymous political writings. He spoke from inside the whirlwind, slashing at whatever menaced the peace and order of Connecticut.

For two years after Jefferson's election the seat of Dwight's operations was the Boston *Palladium,* a journal dedicated to defending clerical influence in politics. During a visit Dwight made to Charlestown in 1800, he devised with Jedediah Morse a new Federalist newspaper to be called the *New England Anti-Jacobin.* To fight Deism and Republicanism, it enlisted the contributions and support of politicians and clergymen enraged at the defeat of Federalism at the polls. The editors sent to every clergyman in New England free copies brimful of political subject matter for sermons. "I think," Dwight wrote to Morse, "New England will be saved from ruin."[23]

Fisher Ames, another founder, wished the *Palladium* to act "fastidiously polite and well-bred. It should whip Jacobins as a gentleman would a chimney sweeper, at arms' length and keeping aloof from his soot."[24] Its language, however, rarely transcends gutter politics; and its tone is vicious. Dwight provided three series of ill-tempered essays, and possibly some poems which cannot with certainty be attributed to him. The *Palladium* was short-lived; its editor resigned in 1803, after which Dwight ceased to contribute. Yet it exerted some political force of its own, extended Dwight's, and earned the hatred of Republicans who, despite his anonymity, baptized Dwight its "Grand Pabulum."

In two series of his essays Dwight attempted to justify clerical participation in government. The first series, consisting of four essays appearing in consecutive issues of the magazine in 1801, anonymously, was addressed "To the Farmers and Mechanics of New-England." By appealing to the plain people, Dwight hoped to show how Republican objections to clerical politics (and to "Pope" Dwight) were ultimately directed against them. Frankly, he argued that political events as deeply affect ministers as other men:

> A clergyman is as much a free citizen as any other man, and therefore as naturally, and deeply interested in the political concerns of his country. His property, though small, is his all, and must as much be defended by the laws of his country as that of his richer neighbours. His personal liberty is dependent on the same principles as that of other men. His family are as dear to him as the families of other men are to them, and both their rights and his own are as valuable and important to him as the rights of any citizen whatever are to himself.[25]

Dwight told his readers that, in addition to their natural social interest, the clergy are often enlightened men, well qualified to deal with politics, which their indifference to political preferment allows them to view impartially. Confident that the whole history of New England argued his case, he claimed that traditionally the "people of New England" adopted the same opinions on political subjects as their clergy, simply because they considered those opinions to be just and right. During the Revolution, the clergy had identified themselves with the people's interests and had issued the first cries for Independence. Dwight ended his call for popular trust in the ministry by identifying the clergy and citizens of New England: infidels and others who can't manage their affairs blame both together, simply for promoting "good order, and a steady course of wise governmental measures."

Dwight continued his bid for renewed clerical power in a series of essays entitled "Farmer Johnson's Political Catechism." The title, welding agricultural, clerical, and political interests, again hints at the importance to the "plain people" of close union between politics and religion. The "catechism," in question-and-answer form, concerns problems of suffrage and religious establishments. Dwight makes no serious attempt to characterize the respondee, Farmer Johnson, who speaks with simple but impersonal dignity as he argues for general, not universal, suffrage, based on property—a minority opinion in 1800. Like the farmer in *Greenfield Hill,* he stresses the intimate relation between property and social good will; and he admits a personal stake in the fate of the clergy:

> Q. How does religion make a man useful to his fellow men?
> A. By rendering him just, sincere, faithful, kind and public spirited, from principle. It induces him voluntarily, and always, to perform faithfully in the several duties of social life . . . all the real good of society springs from the performance of these duties, and cannot exist without them.[26]

Government-supported public worship benefits even the farmer by teaching large groups of people—more effectively than coercive laws and without expense—decent manners, orderly business tactics, and friendliness. Also, the farmer says, government should support public worship because it fosters "attachment in the people to itself," keeping alive a sense of the past in the present which is another source of stability. Dwight denied government the power to dictate or compel religion, but he held it obliged to provide the means and opportunities of worship. Until the government did more than provide the means, he saw no danger of religion becoming an engine of statecraft.

To enforce the "Duty of supporting the New England Institutions," Farmer Johnson recommends severe measures. Public officials should show a knowledge of these institutions and swear an oath to maintain them; judges of the higher courts should once a year explain their nature and importance in charges to the Grand Jury; the clergy should preach an annual sermon "on the settlement of our fore fathers of this Country"; the history of New England should be drawn up in question-and-answer form and "be recited in every school, and by every child"; and the New England institutions should be made the subject of "conversation among all discerning people, and particularly in the presence of the rising generation."

Dwight's conservatism now had a totalitarian ring, and the

charges of popery leveled against him were not inaccurate. New England Federalism had become his religion; New Light orthodoxy, his politics. His desire to restore the government of John Winthrop may seem wishful thinking in a period whose mood opposed state support of religion. Yet in New Jersey only Protestants could hold office; in Delaware, only those professing belief in the trinity; in Pennsylvania, only those professing the divine origin of Scripture. At the cost of whatever restrictions, Dwight would preserve what to him seemed an empirical fact:

> Q. Why ought all these things to be done?
> A. Because New-England has, hitherto, enjoyed more happiness than any country ever enjoyed.

While trying to refashion Connecticut into Zion, Dwight continued his crusade against new ideas. He published in the *Palladium* a group of essays entitled "Morpheus," directed against novel and fanciful schemes of government. Like the blunt question-and-answer format appropriate to "Farmer Johnson," "Morpheus" uses a dream-vision and imaginary voyage appropriate to its dreamer-narrator. This narrator travels to *"The Country of Instruction"* (also called "The Country of Absurdities" and the "Land of Nod"), whose inhabitants spend their lives dreaming while awake and lolling in the capital city of Perfectibility. Tested, their theories prove unworkable.

The Dreamer arrives as a mob howlingly acclaims its newly installed theoretician-king—Godwin. The first essay tests Godwin's notions of personal judgment as a guide to correct action, and his "philosophical benevolence." Dwight presents Godwin as hoist by his own doctrines, which theoretically create freedom but in practice violate human rights:

> "Order," (cried the philosopher) "Order! How can I do you any service; how can I instruct you, unless you keep order, and consent to hear me?"
>
> Order? (murmured a grave man at my elbow) A command of order is a restraint. It is beneath the dignity of man to submit to restraint.
>
> "I beseech you, then, my friends and fellow citizens, to hear me."
>
> We will think of it (replied the grave man.)
>
> We will not think of it (exclaimed a boy.)
>
> Hear him, (roared out a great number of voices.)
>
> . . . .
>
> Fudge, Fudge-man, (growled a brawny fellow.)[27]

Amidst the pandemonium, all of Godwin's ideas boomerang. A disciple of unrestraint pulls Godwin's nose for the fun of it; another picks his pocket for greater need. When Godwin, flushing, asks how the thief knows his need is greater, the thief answers that *"a man's judgment is to be his only guide."* It is an argument that in the guise of "common sense" and release from the "shackles of custom" might have won Dwight in his youth. But in the Jefferson era, religion and tradition seemed to Dwight the only trustworthy guides. He makes Godwin perceive that he must give up either his system or his money. Pigheaded, Godwin gives up his money, and the man of "greater need" dashes off to a cockfight. Inspired by this scene, the mob goes to rape a married woman, exposing the doctrine of "philosophical benevolence," by which Hottentots and Tahitians elicit compassion, while husbands, wives, and children do not. Later they return, broken-nosed and bloody, to exact revenge by tarring and feathering Godwin.

A second essay tests Godwin's idea of common property and the shared fruits of common labor. When Dwight sets the ethereal Godwin against some Yankee farmers, Godwin tries to plough a field, although he has labored only in metaphysical soil, "which he had always taken care of to have smoothed and mellowed to his liking."[28] As a ring of farmers watch, Godwin's trousers snarl the plough, which hits a stone which wallops his shin, knocking him groaning to the ground, where he delivers a speech on Perfectibility. Noting a ploughing-blister on his hand, he cries out in terror that he is smitten by gangrene. The unutopian farmers take over the ploughing and manage it easily. Bleeding and roaring from a second beating by his followers, Godwin limps home, having concluded "after a profound investigation, that a part of mankind had not yet arrived at the proper state of perfectibility to be changed into cosmopolites."[29]

Having seen that intellectual means ineffectual, the dreamer returns, in a related essay, to the city square where Mary Wollstonecraft has begun preaching that women are entitled to all the rights of men. One of the villagers challenges Mary's ideal of the "Manly woman" who deserves the privileges of men because she can "run as fast, leap as high, and as far, and wrestle, scuffle, and box."[30] The villager insists that the first virtue of woman is chastity. She explains Mary's need to find pleasure in the "empty hope of fame" as the result of her unloved and unloving nature. Mary's followers commence wrestling. Mary, thrown into a puddle and significantly philosophizing from the slime, adjures women to seek glory, fame, immortality, and lovers.

Dwight's *Palladium* essays dramatize simple directives: keep women in the home, philosophers away from the pasture, and Republicans out of the administration. More important is the tone Dwight uses in depicting Godwin and his followers as lower-class, city rabble. Mary's gruff voice characterizes her, and all blue-stockings, as rowdy and common, despite her theoretic faith in human "nature." The enemies of Connecticut's plain are not ideas so much as lower-class radicals who seize on ideas to justify taking over the prerogatives of the established. The dreamer's nastily well-bred tone and his politely cynical view of his subjects as chimney-sweepers are in effect a plea to preserve the aristocratic manner of Connecticut life against upward-moving elements in the population.

To Dwight, the end of the century, drummed in by Napoleon and Jefferson, was no cause for celebration. He toasted 1800 with angry horror by publishing in the *Palladium* "The Extract from 'The Retrospect'," part of a longer poem he had written two years earlier. It is apparently the poem he read to William Dunlap in January, 1798, which Dunlap took for a "bitter invective against all frenchmen innovators and infidels."[31] Gruesomely, this poem reminded Dwight's contemporaries of the meaning of France and of the potential of France domesticated in Jefferson. Drawing on the scurrilous language and satanism of the *Triumph,* the hilltop vision of *Greenfield Hill,* and the "rise-skies" rhymes of *The Conquest of Canäan,* Dwight sent a "form" on a "sooty flight" to a summit of the Alps, whence it surveys the spread of vice and the rack of Europe under Napoleon. As the "form" views each European country, it chillingly catalogues the devastations and social deliriums of a world gone mad.

"Infidelity" here means not the philosophy of Voltaire, but the "demons" and "banded hellhounds" of the French Revolution, Danton and Marat, under whom thirty million people have learned to deny God, deify Freedom, and abide in "legal whoredom."[32] Dwight viewed contemporary Europe as outdoing the whole past record of human butchery. Under a pervasive metaphor of conflagration, he describes democracy and infidelity burning houses, looting, raping, murdering, deifying infamy and irreligion. Although the henchman has changed from Chauncy to Marat, the master is still personal (French) liberty, "isolated liberty." Real freedom for Dwight had always to be social, to be consonant with social harmony:

> Can this be freedom? Justice, order, peace,
> Reverence for rule, the sense of general bliss,
> The fear of God, the love of human kind,
> Affections soft, and social tho'ts refin'd,
> The fix'd controul of unresisted laws—
> These in her train celestial freedom draws,
> Wrath, discord, cruelty, and murder fell,
> And snaky Anarchy, the child of hell,
> With all that blaze of fierce, dissocial fires,
> Which isolated liberty inspires—

According to his concept of social liberty, Dwight regarded Napoleon as the offshoot of an unloving and undisciplined society, a self-destructive miscreant who, like Mary Wollstonecraft, "pants for foes, because he finds no friends." What drives the "Corsic Caeser" is neither wealth, victory, nor love of battle, but the cruelties inherent in French life, "Pale Envy," "Fear," "Keen woe," "Ingratitude, a weed each climate yields,/But sown, and cultur'd, in the Gallic fields."

The incendiary atmosphere in France astounded Dwight, but its possible effects on England and America terrified him. He had hoped that England would join America in a worldwide regeneration of religion through missionary work and in a political alliance against France. An England that kept up and extended its Christianity he counted as Europe's sole hope of rebirth. Only in England, "Freedom lives in things, and not in words." Yet he now felt that England too had grown unfeeling and self-indulgent:

> . . . here Corruption pours her sickly stream;
> Here Influence sheds her mild and tainting beam;
> Here power, secure at home, forgets to feel,
> And hears, unmov'd, the tale of distant ill;
> Bids Afric's sons in bloody bondage toil,
> Thrives on the woe, and shines, bedeck'd with spoil.

A morally soft England could not seek renewal from a Jeffersonian America, where "tottering rule stands nodding to its fall" and where people "sigh for blessings of a fairy state."

In 1800 Dwight believed America to be on the brink of a catastrophic, French-inspired civil war; and the signs of it were national opposition to law, religion, and morals. He concluded the poem with a dark vision of a corpse-strewn planet, its "maddening millions" sent to an "untimely grave" in the prelusive fires and chaos of scriptural doomsday. Between Jefferson and Napoleon, Dwight saw little hope for America—or for the world.

CHAPTER 4

The Real America

I *The Second Great Awakening*

DESPITE DWIGHT'S FOREBODING, Jefferson's administration did not start with the spilling of the Sixth Vial. Rather, startlingly, it ushered in a second Great Awakening.

Since 1780 Dwight had bemoaned and raved at the fallen state of American Protestantism, for he had not foreseen that the reaction against skepticism would result in a resurgence of religion. In 1802 about a third of Yale's two hundred and thirty students converted; over thirty entered the ministry. Other revivals followed in 1810 and 1812, spelling the end of Deism at Yale. Benjamin Silliman recorded sunnily how "the trophies of the Cross are multiplied in this Institution. Yale College is a little temple: prayer and praise seem to be the delight of the greater part of the students."[1] The revivals of 1802 were more decorous than those of the mid-eighteenth century but fully as contagious. Although supervised by settled ministers wary of emotional excess, not by a special group of electrifying itinerants, the revivals excited town after town; and, spreading through England and America, they inaugurated half a century of evangelical Christianity.

Dwight's influence in the revivals is problematic. The public hostility to "Pope Dwight," the vehemence with which he incessantly wrote, preached, and taught the overthrow of infidelism, suggest that his influence was great. Yet Yale had witnessed a revival under Stiles, Dwight's predecessor; some Connecticut churches had begun to experience the Awakening even earlier than Yale; and, moreover, the revivals were as much an English as an American phenomenon. It may be, as Edmund Morgan believes, that the view that Dwight's person and writings inspired the revivals can be charged to a later generation of New Englanders who perhaps too readily associated the change in moral climate with the passage from Stiles, whom Dwight called soft on Deism, to Dwight, the scourge of Deism.[2] But whether the revivals in fact traveled to Yale or from it, nearly everyone in Dwight's time felt that he generated them. In no published statement did Dwight credit himself. What satisfaction he felt came from viewing the often chaotic national and international scene with hard-won equanimity: "Gloomy and dreadful as is the aspect of the political horizon," he could write, "the Christian world has already roused itself from the slumber of two centuries."[3]

In this mood of revivalistic optimism, Dwight stopped composing philippics and returned to writing on religious questions. His beliefs, however, had radically changed. For the second Awakening did not "revive" the inwardness of the first, nor the religion of the Puritan forebears; it roused a socially minded Protestantism that had a changed concept of its church. No one had deliberately altered the flavor of Connecticut Congregationalism. The adjustments were imperceptible to those who lived with them, and had been made within the traditional dialectic of the New England theology. For the sake of keeping religious feeling alive during the infidel invasion, many ministers, Dwight among them, gave new prominence to the doctrine of works and less to that of election.[4] They stressed not only the sovereignty of God, but equally the ability of man to win his salvation.

This critical turn from piety to moralism, from being good to doing good, can already be detected in *The Triumph of Infidelity,* with its concern for the social effects of religious doctrines. Quite openly, social considerations direct the many theological works Dwight published between 1800 and 1812. In his *Theology,* four volumes of sermons preached to Yale students, he devised a complete system of divinity in which revelation, not regeneration, became the source of truth and the basis of all thought. Here he codified in doctrinal terms what underlay his attack on Chauncy: he would test all ideas by their social effects—goodness means doing good; virtue, benevolence. Man, while depraved, can be improved by offering him motives such as property and social position. Dwight's Chauncy-like theology thus sanctifies prosperity and status-seeking.

Since Scripture now seemed to Dwight the main guide to personal and social conduct, he tried to prove that its rendering of events is literal. He wrote many essays on the authenticity of the

Bible, chief among them a book-length series of "Lectures on the Evidence of Divine Revelation," published between 1810 and 1813 in the *Panoplist,* a Federalist magazine edited by Jedediah Morse. Into this Cotton Mather-like storehouse of exotic quotes, scientific facts, historical parallels, and chop-logical proofs, he crowded evidence on the probability of the stories of the Fall, the Flood, Cain and Abel, the reality of miracles, and the reasonableness of the Mosaic account of creation. He was also led to reexamine scriptural prophecy; like his religion itself, his millennial views had changed. Following the Revolution, his millennialism was less a reading of Scripture than a call to revolutionary action. His warnings of judgment day were a threat that the suffering saints, the Federalists, would inherit the earth and rule it with Christ. In his 1798 "Crisis" sermon, for instance, he couched the rise of Napoleon in the monitory language of Revelation and warned that only fifty years remained before the new era. But, as the turbulence of 1800 gave way to the revivals, with infidelism all but vanquished, he postponed the millennium to sometime around 2000. He imagined it as the descent of a benign Christianity upon the whole world. In this respect he also approached the position of the hated Chauncy, who regarded his grandfather's chiliasm as nonsense.

Given fresh hope by the revivals, Dwight became newly ambitious of redeeming society; he would Connecticutize the world. He wrote extensively, although hurriedly, on missionary topics and began actively to engage in social work. He sponsored a host of social agencies, many of which were branded as Federalist fronts: the American Home Missionary Society; the Missionary Society of Connecticut; local Sunday School and Bible societies; societies to reform drinking, swearing, dueling, prisons, to aid the poor and the handicapped, and to abolish slavery. He helped establish new religious periodicals, and contributed to them voluminously. Anyone hoping to found a college or seminary, particularly in the Western territories, sought out Dwight, who turned Yale into a placement bureau for Dwight-trained ministers and teachers.

Dwight's sermons of this period record his new social interests. In "The Charitable Blessed" (1810), a typical title, he redrew his picture of the Happy Darky in *Greenfield Hill,* explaining that Negroes, even when emancipated, become "miserable victims to sloth, prodigality, poverty, ignorance, and vice."[5] He emphasized society's obligation to give the Negro not only freedom but also knowledge, property, and "good habits," the staples of the Connecticut Valley. Through his writing, preaching, and social work, he urged on the reorganization of American Protestantism; but, in sum, the basis of this new Protestantism was less the glory of God than the happiness of man. Lacking a sense of regeneration, no longer distinguishing religion from morality, Dwight gave his Calvinism the spirit of its enlightened, humanitarian rivals. He insisted on the paternal kindness of God and on the dignity of man, whose salvation depended not upon saving grace but upon a scripturally sound social awareness.[6] From the point of view of *The Triumph of Infidelity,* Satan had at last won a "friend of virtue."

II Travels

Dwight's new faith represents, perhaps, a travesty of Edwards' piety. Yet, for a while, it composed Dwight's quarrel with himself. He neither saw universal iniquity nor prophesied the Happy Valley; he settled on comfortable realities in plain prose. He had never felt, anyway, that poetry could deal with actualities. During the rest of his life he wrote only two more poems. One was never published. He no longer cared to address a literary audience. The fruit of this new contentedness was his *Travels; In New-England and New York,* his fullest account of American life.

Like all of Dwight's works, the *Travels* was long preparing. Beginning in 1796, the year after he became president of Yale, he devoted his vacations to travel, both for pleasure and exercise. At first, he kept a notebook of his tours to amuse his family; later, he began a regular journal; by 1804, he had enough material for a book. He announced that he was readying the *Travels* for publication. As usual, publication was delayed. He advertised again four years later, then seven years after that, when he blamed the delay on the troubles between England and America; in 1817, after his death, the book was advertised again. Finally in 1821-22, the *Travels* appeared, with maps, in four volumes of nearly two thousand pages.

In collecting material Dwight covered, according to Benjamin Silliman, over twelve thousand miles, mainly on horseback. But his excursions were not his only source of fact or inspiration. In

1800 the secretary of the Connecticut Academy of Arts and Sciences, Simeon Baldwin, sent a circular letter to prominent men of the state, requesting information about local resources and history. He based the thirty-two queries of his letter on a similar scheme used among the Scottish clergy. He asked for details and statistics about such features of local life as topography, forges, mills, timber, agriculture, manufactures, roads, bridges, churches, slaves, diseases, and inns. Hewing to Baldwin's outline, Dwight published (eleven years after Baldwin's request) *A Statistical Account of the Towns and Parishes in the State of Connecticut;* and he worked much of this material into his *Travels*. More important, Baldwin's format trained Dwight's eye; it taught him what to see and to see it statistically. He became a measurer. As a Yale undergraduate, he had relished mathematical problems; now he began calculating bridge-spans, populations, latitudes, congregations, and the quantity of water cascading over Niagara Falls at a given time. Feeling no longer compelled to mythify the republican tone in sumptuous rhetoric, he filled the *Travels* with names, dates, and numbers.

Dwight leavened his mass of hard fact with personal accounts of local history. He fondly details the settlement and development of each little town in the region, each important school; explains place-names; outlines the lives of local leaders and ministers; and estimates with a farmer's eye and a gardener's zeal the quality of the soil. As he tours the New England states, he simultaneously unfolds the history of King Philip's War. He describes local forays, often on a house-by-house basis, introduces some little-known actions, corrects errors about more celebrated ones, and connects events with places in the hope of dramatizing both. In addition to history and statistics, he provides a flow of patter about local curiosities and legends: a letter written by a drowning man; a traveler who crossed a bridge whose planks, mysteriously, had not yet been laid; a hundred-year-old bug, a tale which later found its way to both Thoreau and Melville; the causes of dry rot.

Dwight makes no formal effort to unify this melange, but he does group his jottings into letters, addressed, as Moses Tyler said, "to a dummy called 'an English Gentleman.' "[7] He also gives the journey a geographical logic at odds with the actual chronology of his trips. For instance, to retain the illusion of a single tour, he places a trip to Brookline in 1805 before a trip to New Lebanon in 1799. Otherwise the *Travels* lurch between bald statistics, dry histories, and believe-it-or-nots, hungrily but indiscriminately seizing whatever will prove its underlying propositions about the solidity and enterprise of the New England character. If anything can be said to direct Dwight's zigzag course, it is his abiding love of the Connecticut Valley: "Take it for all in all, I have never seen the place where I could so willingly spend my life."[8]

Dwight writes mainly from outside, with a brusque air of investigation. He arrives in town, counts the schools, measures the bridges, attends a service, and has quickly seen what confirms his belief that New Englanders are sober, pious, industrious, and intelligent. With wearisome sameness, hamlet after hamlet shows him what he wants to see, affording now and then a diverting local hero or curiosity. The deadpan factfinding is only unconsciously relieved, as when a visit with an aged atheist causes Dwight to remark, "It is scarcely necessary to observe, that a man one hundred and sixteen years old, without religion, was a melancholy sight to me." Otherwise, while measuring every bridge, computing every waterfall, Dwight visualizes nothing. His tone is level, reasonable; his style hasty, plain, unstudied, and undistinguished. His statistical paragraphs are often telegraphically brief, his descriptive paragraphs long and sluggish. Practically his only verb is "is."

Yet "is," the stubborn fact, was precisely Dwight's concern. He wrote the *Travels* convinced that, in the accounts of foreign travelers, America had been distorted by misinformation and faulty seeing. Especially in the books of English travelers, an American would have difficulty recognizing his own country: "In some, indiscriminate panegyric, in others, equally indiscriminate censure, and in all, imperfect and mistaken facts and opinions."[9] He intended to give the facts, and to give them in proper perspective. Since Americans already knew the facts and Englishmen did not want to know them, he feared writing a book no American would read and no Englishman would buy. Actually, there had existed since colonial times a lively tradition of corrective literature; for the desire to challenge foreign misconceptions about America had provided the colonists perhaps their first literary impulse. With a triumphant air Dwight exposes literally thousands of errors in page after page of such travelers as the Comte de Volney, Isaac Weld, and the Duc de la Rochefoucault. He twits Weld for observing that American mosquitoes can bite through boots, Rochefoucault for finding a nonexistent Lutheran church in Schenectady, Volney for giving the wrong distance between two towns, the wrong number of log cabins in New England, the wrong height of Niagara Falls—and so on through numberless miscalculations, misspellings, absurdities, and gaffes.

Dwight planned not only to correct these mistakes but also to make clear the powerful cultural prejudices that begot them. More thoughtfully than usual, he concerned himself with cultural psychology, with national images, styles of vision. He wondered, for instance, why Englishmen so often claimed to have observed bad conduct in America. He granted there was much bad conduct to observe; but he admitted no exotically bad behavior that could not be duplicated in London. He explained that English travelers often provoked the bad conduct they discovered. An ingrained sense of privilege made them act "less unassuming, less civil, more distant, more self-complacent and more forbidding" than native Americans of the same class. American innkeepers and store-owners, treated as servants, responded in kind.

Dwight theorized that while this sense of caste caused bad behavior in others, it also nourished false expectations in the traveler. Hostile to America since the Revolution, the Englishman assumed the country was unworthy, so expected to find it dismal: "Great nations are the painters; and always paint themselves riding. Inferior nations are only painted by them; and regularly appear on the picture as ridden." Wishing to see themselves in the saddle, foreign travelers trusted whatever mendacities and old-wives tales confirmed their stereotyped expectations. They listened to untrustworthy, democratic sources: "Few worse informants concerning this country can be found than mere citizens—and yet from these men is unhappily derived most of the information acquired concerning it by foreign travellers." Above all, Dwight found that the visiting Englishman was reluctant to give up his customary enjoyments. He could receive accurate impressions only by a "violation of his habits," and he usually proved unwilling to undergo the pain of conversion.

But even visitors who had the facts, Dwight thought, lacked the sense of the past that would explain them. This need for a perspective was to him related to a conventional esthetic theory, "that the beauty of every fine landscape arises in a great measure from a comparison of the several objects, which compose it; and is made up extensively of the relations, which they bear to each other." Similarly, he believed that the "real" America existed not in the moment, but in an idealized present combining the past and the future: "A country changing as rapidly as New-England, must, if truly exhibited, be described in a manner, resembling that in which a painter would depict a cloud. The form and colours of the moment must be seized, or the picture will be erroneous" (I, iv).

Dwight ascribed the dullness and uncouthness which travelers reported to the travelers' own impoverished historical sense. One must possess the past, he now felt, to know the present. An iconoclastic younger Dwight denounced the prejudices erected by the past, which prevented men from living in the present. Standing on Plymouth Rock, middle-aged, he confessed to feeling a refining "prejudice" as the scene stirred his pride in hallowed New England institutions: holding land in free sociage, universal suffrage, town meetings, the "order, peace, liberty, knowledge, morals and religion" in which New England excels.

Dwight's intimacy with the past gave the *Travels* its best moments. A knowledge of the history of some desolate spot, where an English traveler would have seen nothing, allowed him the kind of epiphany reserved for antiquarians. Amid the emptiness he recalled how a soldier named Gregg, out pigeon hunting, was shot by Indians: "He tried to stand; but speedily fell, and in a moment perceived a huge Indian taking long strides towards him, with a tomahawk in his hand. The savage struck him several blows on the head, drew his knife, cut a circle through the skin from his forehead to the crown, and then drew off the scalp with his teeth" (III, 186).

Englishmen failed to see the real America because to Dwight it was an observation plus a memory. Throughout the *Travels,* voids become shrines; strolls, pilgrimages. Love of place unexpectedly imbues the banal with life. A further injustice was done the country, Dwight felt, by foreigners who lacked an enhancing vision of its future. Standing on the uncultivated land around the White Mountains, he professed to be "transported in imagination" to the near future, when the surrounding gloom will be "measured out into farms, enlivened with all the beauties of cultivation." He required such an imaginative transformation of anyone willing to see the country clearly:

> . . . whatever is rude, broken, and unsightly, on the surface, will, within a moderate period, be levelled, smoothed, beautified, by the hand of man. . . . To do justice to this and every other landscape in the same stage of settlement . . . all these imperfections must be left out of account, and the country exhibited, either as it is in a state of nature, or as it will soon be in a state of complete cultivation.
>
> (II, 129)

Dwight asked, then, that foreign travelers respond imaginatively. Because he thought that America needed to be seen as an incompleted possibility, the *Travels,* for all its air of fact, throws up a mirage. It plies between statistics and calls for generosity. Nothing is as it seems; America must be invested with its past, present, and future before it becomes what it is.

Foreigners also mistake the country, Dwight argued, by failing to see it morally. At the outset he notified readers who would find his account dull, that "adventures, of all kinds, must be very rare in a country perfectly quiet and orderly in its state of society." He felt justified in devoting two thousand pages to men "calmly pursuing the sober business of peaceful life" because, in the moral perspective, this very sedateness cast an honorable light on human nature. Viewed beside the violence of European history, the tranquil sameness of America seemed a thrilling and elevating novelty. A sense of the "glorious contrast" always accompanied Dwight's perception. Some minds, he acknowledged, would take pleasure only in pomp, but "To me there is something far more delightful in contemplating the diffusion of enterprise and industry over an immense forest; where no oppression gives birth to the efforts of man; no sufferings have preceded the splendour; and no sacrifice of life, or even of comfort is necessary to the existence of the *triumph*" (II, 290-91).

The key word of this passage is "contemplation." Dwight asked foreigners not to see America but to contemplate it with good will and with the illuminating awareness of past difficulties, future possibilities, and difference from Europe. Through these rose-colored glasses Dwight could see America in two ways, as a novel contrast to Europe or as a Europe in embryo. Passing the void where men calmly pursued "the sober business of peaceful life," he could take comfort from the fact that here "no oppression gives birth to the efforts of man." Or, equally comforted, he could recall that here some savage "drew off the scalp with his teeth." He could see America's present banality redeeming the gory human past, or he could see its own gory past redeeming its present banality.

But the distortion that in Dwight's view most disfigured the national image was the Theory of Degeneration. It was difficult to correct since it gave all the other distortions a scientific respectability. This theory, derived from Montesquieu's studies of the influence of climate on institutions, was promulgated by the French naturalists Abbé Raynal and the Comte de Buffon. Buffon, who applied physical and biological principles to society, attributed to climate and food the variations in physical characteristics among men. Throughout the American continent he believed he saw a general contraction of nature. He observed, for example, that, because of the climate and geology, Indians had no beards and few children, that livestock transported from Europe to America shrank. Conversely, he declared that American reptiles and insects were larger and fiercer than those in Europe. He made it seem that America's food animals were abnormally scrappy; its animals of prey, abnormally vicious.

Buffon's disciple, Cornelius de Pauw, added that some radical vice in the American climate stunted propagation, conceiving ugly animals, poisonous trees, and syphilitic air. This anti-American biology was incestuous; for each writer borrowed, repeated, and embroidered the other's *similia*: Buffon published his views in 1752, Volney revived them in 1813, Hegel repeated them later.[10] Benjamin Franklin capitalized on such fictions by describing to fascinated English friends the whales that leapt up Niagara Falls. He also confuted them in his "Observations Concerning the Increase of Mankind" (1755). Jefferson, too, in *Notes on Virginia,* offered contrasting evidence of American genius in painting, politics, oratory, and science.

Dwight and Jefferson became, for the moment, allies. For in the *Travels,* reversing Buffon, Dwight amassed evidence proving America fruitful where the naturalists thought it sterile; benign, where they deemed it malignant. He contested the scriptural assumptions of Buffon and de Pauw, who disputed the biblical account of creation by assigning the barrenness of soil, stupidity of the populace, and defectiveness of animal life in America to pestilential swamps and marshes left by a post-Noachian flood.

Dwight countered this with strictly geological evidence based on the smoothness of rock formations in Long Island. Further, he exhaustively tabulated facts and figures that indicated the abundance and health of local trees, fruits, and vegetables, and implied the friendliness of the American climate to animal life. Buffon avowed that the largest American animal was no larger than a year-old calf. Dismissing this as "Laputan," Dwight adduced a thirty-five hundred pound ox, an eight hundred and fifty pound hog, a four-year-old horse seven feet tall, and a Brookfield eagle that "destroyed" a calf. In mammoth charts he compared the weights of specific animals on the two continents, showing those in America to be invariably heftier:

	Europe	America (Vermont)
bear	153	456 lbs.
deer	288	308
porcupine	2	16
weasel	2	12
otter	8	29

. . . . (I, 25)

Possessed of such evidence, Dwight believed one could reverse the theory of degeneration, showing the inhabitants of Europe to be thinner, sicker, and shorter-tailed: "Your continent is grown too old to yield the productions of nature in their full size, while ours, young if you please, certainly vigorous, nourishes them to a state of comparative perfection."

Dwight collected similar evidence to disprove the other half of the theory: whichever American animals were not feeble, the naturalists claimed, were hyperferocious. But Dwight's evidence showed that hardly any wild animals remained in New England; that insects did little damage; that snakes were few, clumsy, and avoidable; and that, altogether, there were "fewer noxious animals of any kind in New England than in most countries on the eastern continent." On the other hand, as in *Greenfield Hill,* Dwight did not care to discredit beliefs about the harshness of the climate. He admitted that the climate of New England was colder and more freakish than that of places of the same latitude in Europe. But he considered it also more healthful. He boasted acquaintance with New Englanders aged one hundred and four, one hundred and seven, one hundred and seventeen, and one hundred and twenty-four; and he calculated that in Europe the chances were fifty-fifty of living to five, in New England fifty-fifty of living to seventeen, while one in four lived to seventy.

Dwight also admitted the inferiority of American crops to European. But he interpreted this as a result of the high cost of cultivation, due to the small labor force, not as the result of a degenerate soil. Lastly, he granted the naturalists a certain wildness of nature in America; but he chided them for being insensitive to its beauty. In the flooded river where atheistic naturalists saw only "terrifying specimens of physical power," Dwight beheld "awful and preeminent grandeur," "the wildernesses created in Arabian tales." And, except for such spectacles, he maintained that nature in New England was "as regular, mild, and undisturbed, as in most countries of the globe."

III *Nature and Society*

From their questionable evidence of diminutive cows and giant gnats, the naturalists divined a comparable sterility or savagery in the whole quality of American life. To argue the independence of genius and climate, Dwight had to retract his own earlier view. In his dissertation on the Bible, he had assigned the genius of the biblical writers to the Mediterranean sun. Now he defined genius as "the power of making mental efforts," and he derived it from personal energy, motives, and social circumstances.

Even on logical grounds Dwight thought the naturalists' argument unsound. If genius did depend on climate, America had every kind; if on heredity, America had every stock. Or if huge mountains and untamed scenery made men wild, the Swiss would be frantic, which they aren't. Thus Dwight found American men not only taller, more agile, and muscular than Europeans but also more quiet, orderly, and sociable. Irritated by naturalistic travelers who considered American women unusually frail, he snipped that they "are certainly less masculine than most of their sex who have visited these states from England." While his own observations confirmed their belief that American women lost their beauty earlier than European women, he attributed this loss not to empoisoned air but to lack of exercise, and parenthetically urged his countrywomen to gargle five times daily with cold water to preserve their teeth. He conceded that frivolous, ignorant, and homely women and vicious men existed in New England, as elsewhere; but what he saw during his travels persuaded him that Americans, on the whole, were energetic and sober, not, as the naturalists jeered, emasculated or savage.

The main exhibit in the naturalists' case was the Indian, whom they considered by turns lazy and murderous. With missionary zeal Dwight pleaded the Indians' capacity for refined emotion. The gist of his long section on Iroquois government and morals is that, in the stereotype of the day, the Iroquois resemble antique Romans for courage and eloquence. What causes the Indian to become "rather a moving vegetable than a rational being" is the lack of "that state of society in which men are able to improve."

Dwight painstakingly traced the Indians' vices—temper, selfishness, coarseness, carelessness, rudeness, and slovenliness—back to their social institutions, independent of soil and climate. He showed how white men living among Indians had become like them. He clinched his argument by reminding Buffon that, if the Indians' vices resulted from their climate, the Indians were not indigenous to America but stemmed, as he and others believed, from Tartar tribes in Asia. While citing the Indians' Roman natures against Buffon, he cited their treacherous personalities against Godwin. The consequences of life lived without restraint he illustrated in a number of harrowing captivity narratives, including Mrs. Rowlandson's: one Indian seated his captive "in an elbow chair upon a table; cut him across the breast and belly; severed his nose and ears and forced them into his mouth." With this incident Dwight notified modern philosophers to "look on, and learn here how romantically innocent, gentle, and amiable, man becomes in this, which they have been pleased to extol as the state of human perfection." He was not hopeful that the Indian character could be reformed, however. He felt that while the Indian's own society made him a "moving vegetable," the white civilization robbed him of motives for glory and made him a shadow. To prevent the Indians' remaining, and feeling, inferior, he urged that they be given tracts of land and segregated.

While naturalists anatomized the Indian character to prove the adverse effects of America's climate on human nature, Rochefoucault and many other travelers used the extermination of Indian tribes to document the harshness and violence of American history. To confute them, Dwight devised his own version of the past; but, although he did not write off such instances of Puritan cruelty as the witch hangings, he read them as he wished foreigners to read America—by the light of the "glorious contrast." He condoned Puritan treatment of the Indians as being more humane than European treatment of other nations, and the Puritan witch hangings as perpetuating European treatment of witches. To show the orderliness in every phase of New England life, he discovered even in incidents he deplored signs of the colonists' good will or of their helplessness to act otherwise. He argued that if the Puritans were overattached to Hebraic law, they had mollified it by reducing the number of capital crimes from one hundred to fourteen; and that, set upon by Indians, they had to defend their lives. Similarly, he saw the American Revolution as the inevitable but reluctant expression of the mutual fears and mutual burdens of rather passive colonists who were in fact more attached to the mother country than to one another. This heritage of good will and order, he believed, survived in the enterprise, learning, and liberty of the present New Englanders, "the only people on this continent who originally understood, and have ever since maintained, the inseparable connection between liberty and good order."

But this liberty, Rochefoucault charged, New Englanders rather professed than practiced. The case of Roger Williams seemed to him typical of the repressiveness, the intolerance, and the wrangling of New England's religious tradition. "The ministers of Connecticut," shot back the author of *The Triumph of Infidelity,* "do not wrangle, and they are not intolerant." Like Cotton Mather and Thomas Morton, Dwight viewed Williams as a threat to the colony's very existence. When not forced to fight for their lives, the ministers of New England had, Dwight protested, been liberal and reasonable. The Connecticut clergy had always proclaimed its toleration, of course, and to argue its case Dwight lavished perhaps a fifth of the entire *Travels* on a patient description of the intricate traditional and legal relations of church and state in New England. He did not regard as signs of a religious establishment the Congregational allegiance required by Yale, or the virtually parochial lower schools which dedicated Saturday afternoons to teaching the Congregationalist catechism embedded in the *New England Primer.*[11] He meant by "religious freedom," rather, that one could belong to what church he chose, but must belong. Only in this way could Dwight maintain that, while a religious establishment existed in Connecticut before the Revolution, it existed no longer. His summary of the certificate law, by which dissenters lodging a certificate of dissent could exempt themselves from church taxes, "so long as they shall ordinarily attend on the worship of the church or congregation to which they shall join themselves," leaves casually unexplored the complicated workings of the law, which made it embarrassing and costly to declare one's dissent.

Besides, on top of denying that a religious establishment existed in Connecticut, Dwight added his opinion that reason and revelation both agree that a legislature may rightfully establish the worship of God: like toppling dominoes, no religion, no morality, no justice, no society. Dwight exorcised the constitutional and legal issues by invoking St. Paul, whom he read as urging legislatures to collect and apportion church funds. As for the presumed intolerance of the clergy, he repeated the homely reasonings of his *Palladium* essays, assigning what influence the clergymen have to popular trust in their office and character; for which, as he always added, they are underpaid. Pointedly, he spared himself the defense of Baptist ministers, even Calvinistic ones, whom he found, as he found most sectarians, ignorant, vulgar, and lower class. Far as he had drifted from Edwards' piety, he wished to show, and perhaps to believe himself, that, excepting a few Unitarians in Massachusetts, the current religion of New England reincarnated the spirit of the apostolic first settlers, providing all worshippers churches within convenient distances, prospering in consonance with "public peace, good order and safety," and, like the thirty-five hundred pound ox, symbolizing the virility and peacefulness of Connecticut life.

Dwight's defense of New England's clergy is the systematic part of an otherwise piecemeal but tireless exposition of Connecticut's institutions. Moving from village to village, Dwight in the *Travels* witnesses a single ideal society, stable without stagnation, progressive without chaos, drawing from him unparagraphed bursts of statistics. The fact, whether population, wealth, number of churches, of roads, of schools, is now the vision; the actual, the ideal; the footnote, the "poetry." Dwight had always detested theory, of course, and had always loved the Connecticut Valley. And now he envisioned the future America composed of small, promising townships, perpetuating the Connecticut ideal by reproducing the exquisite scale of Connecticut life.

Having measured New England, Dwight located its happiness in its moderate size. His model for America was no longer imperial Rome but domestic Switzerland. The small populations represented in Connecticut's local legislatures insured that its laws would affect only its own concerns, while its large representation offered perfect training in public affairs and versed all the inhabitants in local problems. Its institutions thus kept in touch with the lives of its people. Indeed, he felt, it could be administered like a family or congregation. The state, too, he considered small enough so that political candidates could be known personally, but too large to feel the political influence of one man. Salaries for public office were dignified, but no office could be coveted for money alone.

Given the perfect adjustment of individual and social needs, Dwight saw local elections in Connecticut as sharing the decency and quiet of church meetings. He recalled a United States Supreme Court judge who, observing a local election, asked the governor where the rabble were:

> "You see them around you, Sir," said the governor. "Rabble, Sir," said the judge, "I see none but gentlemen and ladies." "We have no other rabble," said the governor, "but such as you see." "You astonish me," replied he. "Why, Sir, when General Washington took the oath of office in the balcony of the assembly-house in Philadelphia, the chief justice, who administered it, could scarcely be heard at the distance of ten feet, on account of the noise and tumult of the yard below. Among the thousands who are present, I do not discover an indecorum. These your only rabble, Sir! Well, I will say, that the inhabitants of Connecticut are the only people within my knowledge who understand the nature of an elective government."
>
> (I, 235)

Dwight believed that, through the familial scale of Connecticut life, the coercion needed to check sinful man had been painlessly institutionalized. At the same time, coercion had been personalized by means of general education. The informed, literate farmers and mechanics fostered stability by keeping an alert skepticism to political and religious novelties. An educated citizenry did for itself the work of a coercive state; its knowledge internalized "that stability which is elsewhere produced by energy in government."

In naming general education and family-sized government as the bases of Connecticut's happiness, Dwight had shifted ground. In

Greenfield Hill, what unites self-interest and public service is the equal descent of property and "Competence." From one point of view Dwight had merely expanded "Competence" to embrace all the activities of government. In Greenfield Hill, no man has too little for existence or enough for dissipation; every man has enough to be unenvious but too little to be complacent. In the Connecticut of the *Travels,* every institution is small enough to be personal and large enough to be effectual, but too large to be bossed and too small to attract bosses. Like the "mediocre" yeomen of Greenfield Hill, Connecticut thrives on a double bind. Because of the scale of its institutions, it can become neither authoritarian nor libertine.

From another point of view, however, the upshot of Dwight's discussion is simply that the state's unique well-being is the creation of wise Federalist-Congregationalist interests entrenched in the schools, churches, and legislatures. Except for the sake of argument, it mattered little to Dwight what produced the happiness of Connecticut: during the depression, economic scarcity; during the revivals, the clergy. Description was explanation enough since his premise was that Connecticut was the finest place on earth, observably and beyond argument. Because he loved his home, his friends, and his work, he saw Connecticut as the nearest achieved expression of pure republicanism.

Occasionally, indeed, for all his ridicule of Buffon, Dwight traces the peace and order of Connecticut to its soil and climate: "people, who live on a pleasant surface, and on a soil fertile and easy of cultivation, usually possess softer dispositions and manners, and feel themselves entitled to a higher character than those, who, from inhabiting rougher grounds, acquire rougher minds, and form coarser habits" (II, 315). The grounds of proof mattered little to Dwight. He would allow any argument, cite any source, that validated by reason or authority what was to him an emotional fact—that nowhere else but in Connecticut could be found "the same strong sense of religion, the same firm moral habits, the same enlightened education of the whole body of the people, the same riveted love of good order, and the same powerful public sentiment."

Because Dwight intensely cared to prove that Connecticut was such a place, but not how he did so, his evidence that its institutions do create happiness, that its inhabitants are not savage, is abundant, factual, and not very persuasive. Its domestic character makes charmingly vivid his sense of the safety and comfort of the Connecticut Valley. He made it a policy, however, never to cite his sources; and he seems to have consulted mainly his own wishes. All his evidence has a suspect definiteness. He knows, for instance, that from "one-half to two-thirds" of New Englanders sleep year round without locking their doors, that no house in New Haven has been entered in sixteen years, that only five duels have been fought in New England, that during eight years of Revolution only one man was murdered, that fewer capital crimes are committed in New England than in any other place on earth except Scotland.

Dwight's explanation for what violence has erupted is equally fanciful. The one Weathersfield man who went berserk and axed his wife and children turns out to have been a Deist. Other local disorders were hatched abroad; for, in his manichean version of regional history, all the inhabitants of New England lived upright, God-fearing lives until 1755, when for the first time infidel British troops mingled among them. Further disorders resulted from the Revolution, when young soldiers met Frenchmen; and, although the region began to recover after the peace of 1783, from "France, Germany, and Great Britain, the dregs of infidelity were vomited upon us at once." The French Revolution then corrupted New England youth who desired to be fashionable, while infidels capitalized on the traditional free inquiry of a New England education.

Dwight's sense of periodicity is compounded of John Homely's contempt for foreigners, Farmer Johnson's respect for clerical power, and his own charge that foreign travelers distort the country by creating the bad behavior they find. Dwight found firmer evidence of the state's perfect order and mildness in its own laws and institutions: its few capital offences (twelve, including bestiality and sodomy), its universal establishment of education, its permission to carry arms, which in Europe, he pointed out, would constitute a danger to the state.[12] But, except when discussing laws and institutions, he did not interpret his "evidence." Casually noted in brief paragraphs, paragraph after paragraph, the single ax murderer and the huge hogs speak for themselves, declaring the comfort and health of Connecticut life.

Less consciously, however, Dwight's love of permanence discovered for him an omnipresent symbol of order—the New England house and its grounds. This "sprightly, cheerful" presence was to

Dwight the image and substance of the good life. By suggesting the goodness, harmony, and friendliness of its inhabitants, it completely answered all the criticisms of Buffon and Rochefoucault: "A succession of New-England villages, composed of neat houses, surrounding neat school-houses and churches, adorned with gardens, meadows, and orchards, and exhibiting the universally easy circumstances of the inhabitants, is, at least in my own opinion, one of the most delightful prospects which the world can afford" (I, xv).

Dwight had always considered the love of property indispensable to sound morals, reconciling lawless man to government. Now he equated neat houses with that exquisite adjustment of personal pleasure to social responsibility which epitomized for him the Connecticut Way: "the intent of settling in them, is not merely to acquire property; but to sustain the relations, perform the duties, and contribute to the enjoyments of life." The white clapboard house expressed Dwight's essential morality.

Throughout the *Travels* Dwight read architecture as a seer reads entrails for omens of the future. He scrutinized each building to see how the people regarded themselves. Careful construction signified a love of place, portending permanence; plainness, a lack of envy, portending social harmony; foliage, closeness to the soil, portending hardihood. Beauty he always interpreted as an expression of social consciousness. Revisiting Lake George in 1807, after a previous visit in 1792, he gazed admiringly at a growth of neat and handsome houses, because they boded a stable future. (Nearby Saratoga augured ill, he thought, since its waters encouraged drunkenness by preventing "the malignant effects of repletion.")

While Dwight favored the white clapboard house, he allowed a more splendid style for public buildings. Again his motives were not esthetic but social, for he believed that the sight of fine things in society prompted men to act well. Stone public buildings particularly impressed him as evidence of permanence and self-respect. In the *Travels* he studied the public buildings of Boston and New York with great care, affording pages-long technical descriptions to the porticos, columns, entablatures, free-stone bases of hospitals, asylums, prisons, and churches. He entered each minute measurement with Delphic solemnity, as a telltale projection of the people's self-regard, thus of its promise.

"The effect of a framed or stone house is immense on the tranquillity, power, and refinement of the builder" wrote, not Timothy Dwight, but Ralph Waldo Emerson in *Society and Solitude.* A unique sense of cultural topography connects the two men and their differing eras. They saw, as Emily Dickinson said, "New-Englandly." Each conceived society only in terms of himself, his house, and the people who visited with him. One might trace changes in Dwight's thinking about America simply by observing his changing ideals of a homesite. The youthful nationalist of "America" called for "temples starr'd with gems and roof'd with gold," but the spokesman for Connecticut contented himself with the "sprightly, cheerful" New England house. In Europe, middle-class architecture was not meant to bespeak its country's values or its people's will. European houses, Dwight thought, were chosen for advantages of trade or status. In seeing the domicile as a symbol of his culture's highest hopes, Dwight returned to the domesticity of Anne Bradstreet, lamenting in the ashes of her burned house the loss of all good. He looked forward to Louis Sullivan's sense that what people are within, buildings express without. For in the "sprightly, cheerful" clapboards of Connecticut, Dwight saw not merely a "glorious contrast" to European pomp and infidelism but more glorious signs of progressive and orderly people.

The hundred houses of the *Travels,* their white paint and foliage artlessly though lovingly noted, manifest how deeply on Dwight's mind was impressed the interrelation of order and ownership. Like Yeats's Tower, they are final, long-evolving symbols of his innermost convictions.

IV *Change*

If the white clapboard house roused Dwight's hopes, the log cabin sank them. A corollary to his hope that neat houses would breed respectable people was his fear that "if a poor man builds a poor house, without any design or hope of possessing a better, he will either originally, or within a short time, conform his expectations to the style of his house." In the log cabin he foresaw impermanence, anarchy, sloth; and any other iniquities he identified with lower-class democracy. When he describes cabins in the *Travels* and explains their construction, he invariably raps them as "certainly no ornaments to the landscape." Walking by some shanties in Cambridge, he revealingly fantasizes that the tenants subsist off Harvard, and that the wife takes in washing and mending ("How far it is applicable in fact, I am not informed.") He considered it inauspicious that the trees of western New York are frail, for in sparse woods he saw flimsy buildings, and in them divined infidels and democrats.

Behind Dwight's bourgeois air of appraising the furniture lies a search for clues to cultural change. The log cabins showed him what sort of place America was becoming. And his test of whether Connecticut could exist in that kind of place was the fate of the frontier, which he regarded as both a national hope and a national disgrace. By means of the movement to the West, he hoped to plant New England's institutions across the whole country, but he also feared that in the wilderness they would not take hold. A West settled according to mob rule, irreligion, and transiency would make Connecticut ashamed of its Union and might threaten its own good order.

Generally, Dwight disliked the pioneers. He found their politics Republican, their religion unorthodox when existent, and their temperament favorable to quackery. At first he blessed the emigrations for draining off local malcontents; and, had the pioneers' political influence not been felt nationally, he would probably have ignored them. But wilderness Vermont became a democratic outpost in 1804. Moreover, as Dwight lamented in the *Travels,* although every Connecticut farmer could read and reason, "improvement" in the state had been sluggish, for the furor of emigration kept its population at a standstill. Because many recognized the future of the West, could afford its cheap lands, and, after 1812, could readily get to them, the population of many Connecticut towns was larger in 1790 than in 1821.[13]

Dwight's description of the frontier in the *Travels* betrays these mixed hopes and fears. His offhand sketches of frontier ways leap out from the enveloping sobriety of his statistics with sputtering contempt. He depicts the new territories as wilderness Gomorrahs, tropical compounds of regional and racial types holding explosively diverse opinions, failing to insist on formal declarations of religion, bossed by speculators and adventurers, wallowing in "alienation from religion, and dissoluteness of manners." Peddlers are wanderers, "accustomed to no order, control or worship"; fishermen and lumberjacks are "dissolute"; and new settlers generally are often "roving, disorderly, vicious" men whose licentiousness is abruptly "set loose."

Yet, along with this dread of an orgastic Maine or Ohio, the *Travels* argues a quite opposite hope. Guided by his theory of challenging "motives," Dwight speculated that people who move from old to new settlements may display unexpected talents. Their novel circumstances may call forth genius, and their new property may inspire love of order.[14] Older settlements provide few motives to exertion "because everything, which prompts to effort, was already in the possession of others"; but in new settlements everything lies equally open to all. Dwight both feared and counted on the individualism of the frontier. It could beget license; or, by acquiring property as the reward of its enterprise, it could beget order.

What would decide the outcome, Dwight proposed, was the ability of the "New England education and habits" to prevail on the frontier during its settlement. He took some hope from Yale's missionary activities to the West. But, like many other Congregationalists, he worried that Congregationalism would not thrive in unformed communities. Its atmosphere of respectability, learning, and piety might content only an educated middle class of New England origin. In fact, the Congregational pattern of autonomous church government did not fill the need of a loose frontier society for a strong, central church polity.

While concerned that Congregationalism might flounder, Dwight eyed the Western, Jeffersonian Methodists and Baptists as politically dangerous and as infectiously ignorant. They seemed to him a baleful influence on the new settlements, where the people of Connecticut had many relatives and friends. In an "Address, to the Emigrants from Connecticut," published in 1816, he exhorted his friends and neighbors to carry with them to the frontier and to plant there the New England institutions of learning and religion: "Long established institutions have a mighty influence over the whole population of old settlements. When these institutions and habits are good, they operate as so many checks, upon the corrupt propensities of our nature. Every man acts under the public eye, and feels a responsibility, which restrains sinful inclinations, and serves to regulate his daily deportment."[15]

Alone in the wilderness, this public conscience withdrawn, a man could "set loose" with impunity. Dwight urged his neighbors, a common stock he addressed with the closeness of a Puritan community, to provide from the beginning religious instruction for their children, Bible reading, Sabbath observance, and the establishment by public support of a settled church and ministers, whatever the sacrifice in money. To neglect religious institutions on the frontier, he warned, "is *death.*"

What else might decide the character of the frontier, Dwight believed, was the pattern of its settlement. He wished the change from wilderness to settlement to occur in steps formulated to ensure orderliness. He proposed three stages, resembling the "three descents" of social change in *Greenfield Hill;* but both patterns are modeled on the theory of the cyclical rise and fall of empires. The first stage of settlement is the planter who clears ground and builds a house. Doing without neighbors, he is uplifted by rich crops and kept healthy by hard work. The second stage begins when neighbors arrive; the planter remains energetic, but becomes sociable too. He builds a permanent house, buys good furniture and clothing, and acquires through them better manners. The third stage consists of regular society. In this ideal form of settlement, progress and order keep pace. The settler refines and civilizes what in turn refines and civilizes him. He does not aim at grabbing land but at founding a community.

This Dwight called "settling in the New-England manner." He distinguished carefully between socially minded "settlers," "planters," or "farmers" and merely adventurous "pioneers" or "foresters." When the pioneer or forester moves to the backwoods, he becomes "less and less a civilized man." Misanthropic and shiftless, he ambles continually west, buying farms and clearing lands, but lighting out as soon as settlers arrive. These settlers do the real work of civilization: "the strong columns of civilized men regularly push before them these Arabian troops; and will, at no great distance of time, follow them to the Pacific Ocean." Dwight's hope was that the farmers would forget feuds and divisions and, building towns, "assume the general New-England character." Aspiring towns nearby would emulate those with "settled worthy settlers" by building churches, calling qualified clergymen (and paying them well), and uprooting infidelity, thus planting New England's "freedom, energy, learning, good order, and religion."

Dwight found both historical and contemporary evidence of the success of "settling in the New-England manner" and of the danger of settling otherwise. New England itself, he pointed out, enjoyed from the beginning the third stage of settlement; for no real gap had existed between the first excursion to the wilderness and the complete population. But, while New Englanders had settled by small towns, in the "village manner," the other English colonies had settled in scattered plantations, which had shaped adversely the character of their settlers. Cut off from churches and schools, and from "that daily intercourse which softens and polishes man," they became coarse and insular. Their manner became "distant, rough, forbidding, gross, solitary and universally disagreeable." They approached other men with a "rustic sheepishness or a more awkward and provoking impudence." New Englanders, by contrast, settling in villages, each with its own church and school, became neighborly, social beings who "converse; feel; sympathize; mingle minds; cherish sentiments; and are subjects of at least some degree of refinement."

Dwight found a more contemporary instance in the planting of New York state. He observed that the inhabitants of the New England-type settlements of Suffolk were distinguished from those in the pioneer-type settlements of western New York by "their names, their pronunciation, their manners, their attachment to the education of their children, their intelligence, their morals and their religion." Moreover, he found that the alien, democratic element of Suffolk, "the coarse and protruberant lives of the clumsy and insolent multitude" were being refined by the example of the New England element, the "refined sentiments and conduct of the small number." But in western New York he could find no enterprise, cultivation, churches, schools, manners, intelligence, morals (or, handily, sturdy trees). New York City, with its mixture of New Englanders and mostly illiterate Europeans, seemed to him more hopeful; for he believed that the "small number" would transform the rest, who inevitably would "soon be so entirely amalgamated with those from New-England as to be indistinguishable."

Despite his hope that the New England character would prevail, Dwight feared that the boundless, unruled frontier would "set loose" man's desire to be masterless. His shocked description of the Western settlements seems to confirm rather than to deny Montesquieu's studies of the influence of climate on institutions, and the naturalists' view of the "savage character" of the Americans. Indeed, the *Travels* is far from being a wholehearted defense of American life. Working on his book between 1796 and 1815, Dwight recorded his always changing feelings about the country without bothering to resolve them. Probably he wrote those portions of the *Travels* unfavorable to the American West and South around 1812, when he saw the possibility of a split in the Union. As he rearranged the chronology of his trips, however, his criticisms of the West and South became scattered through the whole, making a typically confused effect.

The result is a monumental anachronism. The *Travels* alternates elation and alarm, the discordant moods of the second Awakening and the War of 1812. Out of these moods grows a single theme—that everything good in America is owing not to the land, to the climate, or to the soil but, quite strictly, to the institutions and traditions of New England. Dwight's argument that Europeans should view America generously amounts to seeing New England first; better still, Connecticut; best, its Congregationalist-Federalist leadership.

Throughout the *Travels* the hopeful facts of 1802 are ringed round, therefore, by the doubts of 1812. Dwight's need to distinguish farmers from pioneers, Greenfield Hill from Ohio, Connecticut from America, questions the value of the thirty-five hundred pound ox as a specimen of American vitality. Dwight treated as another distortion those travelers who view America as a single place. He resented their crediting Connecticut with Western and Southern vices. The customs, manners, and morals of the states "at the southern and western borders of the Union," he insisted, are "to a great extent, absolutely unknown in New-England, and the stories concerning the inns, the churches, the ministers, the horse-racing, the cock-fighting, the gambling . . . are as little applicable to New-England as to Old England and in most instances much less."

Dwight compiled statistics to confirm this new "glorious contrast." In Connecticut dwell one hundred and eighty-nine ministers and two hundred and nine congregations, while in all the states south of New England there are only four hundred and thirty congregations and two hundred and forty-two ministers. In Connecticut, every person can hear the Gospel and observe the Sabbath, while southward a number of people "several times as great as the census of Connecticut, have scarcely heard a sermon or prayer in their lives." Indeed, he sometimes employs against the Southern and Western territories the dark biology of the naturalists themselves: in Europe, the chances are fifty-fifty of living to five; in New England, fifty-fifty of living to seventeen—but there is twice as much chance of reaching forty-five in New England as in Georgia. Thunderstorms are "much more violent as we advance southward," one Charleston storm lasting four days.

While separating New England from the rest of the Union, Dwight solicited a privileged friendship between New England and old. He made it clear, again most probably in the latest portions of the *Travels,* that the New England institutions he glorified were made in England, that the genius of the New England way descends from the first settlers, who were born in England. He claimed to have traced to England by "irresistible evidence" New England's love of liberty, its desire for strong government, its sense of friendliness and mutual help, its common decency, and its union of obedience to law with individual self-interest. For himself, he admitted he would "find no difficulty in worshipping under a conscientious and evangelical minister" of the English church or in conducting a service according to its liturgy for those "who seriously chose it." Having begun his *Travels* to persuade foreigners to give up their "customary enjoyments" so as to experience the novelty of America, he ended it with assurances that England was just like Connecticut.

That the New England institutions would spread to the West, these notes of discord reveal, was rather Dwight's hope than his belief. For by 1812 he agreed with Montesquieu that a republic might not be able to exist in a large territory. He also found the character of the Union such that Connecticut could not live with it. Although he visited Philadelphia, he significantly failed to include an account of it in his book. In limiting the *Travels* to New York and New England, he embraced a single region that, joined in character and institutions, had a chance of staying together should the Union dissolve. New Yorkers and New Englanders could find in "their local situation, soil, and climate; in their religion and political systems; in their arts, literature, and science, in their manners and morals, in their health, energy, and activity, ample, perhaps peculiar sources of national greatness and prosperity." Dwight began his *Travels* by ridiculing those naturalistic philosophers who observed throughout the American continent a general contraction of nature. Before he got through he saw with his own eyes America shrink to New England.

CHAPTER 5

Years of Recompense

I *Decisions*

THE *TRAVELS'* joyous statistics and hopefully neat houses were illusory. Its fretful undertones were prophetic. With the War of 1812 Dwight lapsed into a depth of gloom darker even than his horror at the end of the century. In his "Discourse . . . on the Public Fast" (1812) he announced: "At no time, since the deluge, has the situation of the human race been so extraordinary; the world so shaken; or its changes so numerous, sudden, extensive, and ominous."[1] It was doomsday again.

Dwight had long insisted that New England would never enter a war against old England. As early as 1793, praising Washington's proclamation of neutrality, he had calculated that "sooner would ninety-nine out of a hundred of our inhabitants separate from the Union, than plunge themselves into such an abyss of misery."[2] Now, in 1812, he showed that he meant it. As the leading Federalist in his state and its most eminent public figure, he gave the support of his national prestige to the Hartford Convention as it moved toward secession. As the religious revivals changed Dwight the Calvinist into Dwight the enlightened Protestant, the War of 1812 changed him back. It renewed his dormant chiliasm. He gave scriptural prophecies a fatalistic contemporary reading, and again in rumbling apocalyptic language he cited Deism, infidelism, and the French Revolution as causes of the war.

Completely and unblushingly he once again identified hard religion with good government. Again he became the inheritor of the Puritan tone. "Shall we confide," he asked, "in Egypt?" But he no longer felt like the author of *The Conquest of Canäan,* and Egypt was France now, not England. Having written America its first epic poem he began, on the Puritan note, composing its dirge:

> Turn your eyes to *Europe.* Where are the republics, which once flourished, there, in freedom, virtue, and happiness? *Their pomp is brought down to the grave, and the noise of their viols. The worm is spread under them, and the worms cover them.* . . . Where are her cities? *They have been searched with candles.* . . . Look at her fields: they are whitened with human bones, and drenched in human blood. . . . *It is the day of the Lord's vengeance; the year of recompenses for the controversies of Zion. The earth is utterly broken down; the earth is moved exceedingly.*

By once more adopting the persona of the Puritan Jeremiahs, Dwight was warning his audience to reclaim its original historical personality, to listen to its ministers, not to its politicians.

The government's threat of war outraged Dwight for two reasons. It promised to end the effective association of American and English missionary societies in worldwide evangelical effort. But unthinkably worse was the chance of American alliance with France, the "charnal-house of Atheism." On this possibility Dwight confessed his feelings to be "inexpressible." Such an alliance, he protested in his "Discourse," was to "chain living health and beauty, to a corpse dissolving with the plague . . . the horrors of war, compared with it, are mere amusement." To this already awesome prospect he added the possibility of Britain's landing ten thousand black troops in East Florida. Calling on his audience's racial guilt, he warned, "he who remembers the state, extent, and feelings of our black population, and calls to mind that GOD is just, will look at this object with a pained eye, and an aching heart."

Like a seventeenth-century New Englander, Dwight had begun viewing events as a divine punishment of communal sins. His writings of 1812, confessions of communal guilt, are throwbacks from the Enlightenment to the seventeenth century. They beg for communal redemption by acknowledging and repudiating New England's part in the creation of the Union. Tracing the present crisis to the nation's godless beginnings, Dwight placed before his audience the choice of sedition or damnation: "We formed our Constitution without any acknowledgement of GOD; without any recognition of his mercies to us, as a people, of his government, or even of his existence. The Convention, by which it was formed, never asked, even once, his direction, or his blessing, upon their labours. Thus we commenced our national existence under the present system, without GOD." The current results of this unblessed Union, Dwight claimed, were unprecedented covetousness, drunkenness, falsehood, murder, rigged elections, party spirit, office hunting, and the Republican administration. More than three million Americans, he declared, now live without regular worship of God. America had become *"a smoke in the nostrils* of JEHOVAH."

Dwight confessed his own guilt by denouncing his youthful idealism. His retractions appear in the embittered "Decisions" he delivered to Yale students in 1813-14, published in book form in 1833. Like Ezra Stiles, he openly discussed delicate social and political problems with the senior class, arming young Connecticut men with proper attitudes toward such questions as "Would a Division of the Union be Beneficial?", "Ought Religious Tests to be Required of Civil Officers?", "Would a Permanent Navy be Beneficial to the United States?" While indoctrinating his students, he reviewed and repented his youthful folly: "The song 'Columbia' which I wrote in the army," he confessed to them, "was the production of enthusiasm arising from the pleasing idea of having this country become the refuge of the oppressed. No men leave their country (with a very moderate exception) but worthless characters. . . . All now love the spot of ground where he was born and bred."[3] Where the republican author of "Columbia" had seen America as the last refuge of virtue for mankind, where the more skeptical Federalist had questioned the special treatment of immigrants, the apostate wished to stop immigration altogether. All Europeans now seemed to him ignorant, prejudiced, and bound to bring with them shiftlessness, pauperism, vice, a spy-system, indecent books and songs, and a passion for war.

Dwight did not stop at immigration. Where the Yale tutor urged a Declaration of Independence, where the Northampton preacher questioned the results of the war, his own most severe critic denounced the Continental Army as "revolting" and "shocking," as "bad men" who would "talk of butchering men, as if they had been butchers, talking about slaughtering an ox,"[4] men who had infidelized the country and reduced the salaries of ministers: "I have not the same views of dependence which many have. I believe that God made men necessary to each other, in order that a sense of our dependence might lead us to treat one another as we ought."

Where the author of "Columbia" saw an imperial America enriched as "the east and the south yield their spices and gold," the isolationist deplored any extension of American commerce and manufactures as exposing it "to the vice, disease and disorderly spirit to which manufacturing nations are subject." Where the epic poet hoped for an America united in manners, morals, and religion, where the traveler hoped that the New England manner would spread to the West, the budding Anglophile bowed to an America where "the inhabitants of distant parts have little more intercourse with each other than if they lived in different countries."

Far from thinking continentally, Dwight now opposed any extension of the Union. It could only weaken the already crumbling government and create not new Americans but new aliens: "the inhabitants of the regions about the Rocky Mountains are as much strangers, and as likely to be enemies, as those at the Mississippi." Local partialities and antipathies, Southern congressmen publicly insulting Eastern states, Jefferson's destruction of Northern commerce through his embargo—these seemed to Dwight insurmountable blocks to national feeling—blocks, one should add, that his own intense localism did nothing to discourage. He never went to the treasonable extreme of calling on his students to end the Union, for he feared that civil war would invite foreign intervention, and he preferred living in mutual disharmony to living under foreign rule. Yet he expected that the country would split of its own fractures: "I fear we may not stand long. I shall not see our fall, but you may."

Nor did Dwight wish his students to think that the American experiment had failed entirely. Having lost, however, his nationalistic fervor, he abandoned altogether the cyclical view of history which had flattered it. That view had provided his favorite metaphor of rise and fall, allowing him to see America as the place where "Empire's last, and brightest throne shall rise" (*Conquest*, X, 555). Now he invoked a unilinear conception of history in which he counted the discovery of America a "great impulse" within the history of the West, and a contribution to the general improvement of the human mind since Noah. America had thus benefited humanity, if not Americans. Among its benefits he numbered the increase in the population of Europe, for Americans had given to the world increased means of subsistence. America had added much to science, and by improving the art of navigation reduced the risk of ocean travel. It had sped the revival of Christianity and had improved the humane character of men. Through its investigations of the Indian, it had shed light on the common origin of mankind. Meaningfully absent from this list of American achievements was the system of government that Dwight had praised and once codified in couplets. Of that government he was no longer the advocate.

II Inchiquin's Letters

By denying America a special, providential place in history, Dwight hoped to prepare his students to look at England in a new and filial way. At the same time, he wished Englishmen to see that Connecticut differed from the rest of the country. That England might not be ready to understand prodigal Connecticut should have been clear to him from his experience in combating English misconceptions about America. It was not clear to him; he received the news with pain and surprise.

Charles Jared Ingersoll had published anonymously in 1810, *Inchiquin, The Jesuit's Letters,* a novel defending American culture as seen by a fictional traveling Jesuit. Later the book was damned by the *Quarterly Review.* The reviewer, possibly Robert Southey, made it evident that England was far from wanting the privileged friendship on which Dwight had publicly staked his reputation. Admitting that he had not read the review, but humiliated by its well-publicized enmity, Dwight issued in 1815 an anonymous, one hundred and seventy-six page reply, *Remarks on the Review of Inchiquin's Letters.*

For his rebuttal, Dwight adopted a new persona, plainly called for by his new stance. In the *Travels* he declared himself "an American, a republican, and a Presbyterian." Now he announced, "I am a federalist, a *New Englander;* a Yankee."[5] While no longer claiming to be an American (the book was signed "By an inhabitant of New-England"), he also no longer claimed to be addressing all Englishmen. His title specified that his remarks were "Addressed to the Right Honorable George Canning, Esquire," an English Tory whose newspaper, the *Anti-Jacobin,* had inspired the *Palladium.* Dwight's original "glorious contrast" had set off England from America, Cooper's Hill from Greenfield Hill. Later it balanced America against France, then America against Connecticut.

Now Dwight lined up the best elements in England and America, Tories and Federalists, against the worst elements, lower-class English radicals and defenders of Madison and Jefferson. Much less hesitantly than in the *Travels,* he severed Yankees from Americans and tried to demonstrate the continuity of Anglo-Yankee culture. The least visionary and "poetic" of Dwight's works, the *Remarks* openly admits serious, existent faults in America. As its focus is narrower than the *Travels,* its tone is more passionate, sometimes hysterical. With its references not to Pope, Addison, and Washington, but to Lord Byron, Francis Jeffrey, and James Madison, it has the ring of a new age.

Dwight's implicit plea is that the best elements in England and America should not allow the worst elements to divide them. Accordingly, he compliments England as a bastion of anti-Jacobinism, a "barrier against the ruin of the world," siding with Canning against the "Corsican Cyclops" and praising the "exalted design" of England's effective missionary societies. To his English readers he wished to say candidly what in the *Travels* he only hinted: America *was* savage and unstable, but New England was not. He frankly avowed his own repugnance toward "cunning" Jefferson, the "Master" of "weak" Madison. If hostile to England, he said, both "have been less hostile to you than to us." He absolved Connecticut from any part in the war, which he explained as the result of Madison's lust for reelection and of the greed of Western and Southern states: of Georgia's wanting Florida so as to prevent its becoming an asylum for runaway slaves, of Tennessee's wanting to control the Mobile River, of Kentucky's hunger for Indian lands, of Virginia's wishing to perpetuate its dynasty.

To prove that the demagoguery and greed of Kentucky or Virginia had "no existence north of *Maryland,*" Dwight reworked some of the statistical material from his *Travels.* He showed that in New England before 1812 only eight duels were fought, two by "servants," one by "West Indian youths," and so on (lower-class duelists or foreigners completing the list, which omits his own notorious cousin, Aaron Burr); that American judges were forced by Jefferson to be dependent on the executive branch, but that in Connecticut "the injury naturally derived from this source, has not been felt"; that fighting and gouging exist in the South, but not in New England.

While emphasizing the mutual interests of old and New England, however, Dwight cautioned his conservative audience that, if England continued to mistake Connecticut for America, real alienation would result. As a token of his own willingness to separate English Jacobins from Englishmen at large, he imputed the mistake to the quarterly reviewers. In New Haven Billingsgate he branded them as lower-class radicals, "men like Bonaparte," "bankrupts," "*knots of imprisoned critics,*" "ebullitions from inmates of the *Fleet, Kings bench,* and *Newgate,* prisons," "base and despicable hirelings, employed to aid the dirty purposes of a dirty bookseller." To further suggest why New Englanders and amiable Englishmen should discount the reviews, he charged, traditionally enough, that the reviewers do not read the books they pan, that their favorable reviews are mere puffs of friends or of their own works, and that the typical review is "partly made up of the despicable flattery of Toad-eaters, and partly of the snaky virulence of anonymous hatred." One recalls that, like *The Triumph of Infidelity,* the *Remarks* appeared anonymously. Always best on infighting, Dwight did not care to abide by the "Decision" he had handed down to his Yale seniors that anonymous publications should be forbidden.

Dwight's tough tone assured Yankee readers that they could resume close ties to England without eating humble pie. Less by glorious contrast than by gloating comparison, Dwight found for every Western or Southern American vice an English equivalent, usually from lower-class life. Sometimes his pained surprise at English ingratitude makes it seem that he is again invoking his initial "glorious contrast" between England and America. He argued that the American slave system was no worse than the slavery of the West Indies or the prison ships of Liverpool; that Jefferson, however vicious, never sacrificed his own daughter, as James II did; that the demagoguery practiced from the stumps derived from John Wilkes and Charles Fox; and that the election to parliament of (Sir Mark?) Sykes, who starved a million people in India, made backwoods government seem judicious: "Do you believe, that any scoundrels in the *American* Congress are greater scoundrels than these; or that any orator of a stump in the Southern States, or any backwoodsman in *Kentucky, Ohio,* or

Tennessee, ever deserved to be hanged half as many times?" (28-29). Beside the American mob he set the comparable women of Coventry, standing on barrels, "like the American orators," climbing street railings, passing the bottle, and striking "other positions of the like delicate nature . . . *with a drunken crowd.*"

Dwight capped his comparison with some new statistics. He computed the relative sobriety of America and England. In 1810, by his figures, thirty-three million gallons of "ardent spirits" were imported or manufactured by the 7,289,903 inhabitants of America:

> Dropping the fraction, and stating the number of inhabitants at seven millions, the number of gallons, consumed by each individual, will, at an average, be rather more than four and a half; or (as half drink no ardent spirits,) rather more than nine to each individual in the remaining half. The quantity of Wine, consumed in this country, is not so much as a fourth of the quantity of ardent Spirits; and that of Ale and Porter is trifling in its amount. Two gallons to an individual, of both, will be an ample allowance. We have, then, rather more than eleven gallons of strong drink to each individual in the United States; and 108 gallons to each *Londoner;* viz. nine gallons of ardent Spirits to the *American,* and twentytwo to the *Londoner;* one gallon and a half of Wine to the *American,* and sixteen to the *Londoner;* half a gallon of Ale and Porter, to the American, and seventy to the Londoner. (89)

This farfetched brew of fact, half-fact, and guesswork boils down to the proposition that, if good-intentioned Englishmen would not mistake stumps for clapboards, Dwight would not confuse Jacobin reviewers with Englishmen. Wishing to pacify without seeming to appease, to be friends but not inferiors, and simply irritated, Dwight sometimes sounds again like "our American poet."

The special interest of Dwight's *Remarks,* however, is its defense of American literature and culture. The thirty-odd pages it devotes to the subject revamp material from the *Travels* and the *Decisions;* in the following discussion the three works are considered as one in order to reveal how Dwight's literary views had changed since his youth. What provoked Dwight to defend American culture in his *Remarks* was such a blunder as he quoted from an English review: "The President of *Yale College* talks of a *conflagrative brand,* and President *Jefferson* of *belittling* the *productions of nature*" (139). Nothing would have stung Dwight more, or made him feel more misunderstood, than to find himself paired with Jefferson under a single blanket.

Like the rest of the *Remarks,* the section on American culture serves to divorce Connecticut from America and to point out the harmony existing between the best-thinking elements of Connecticut and of England. In discussing the American language, Dwight showed that these elements shared not only common sentiments but also a common tone. He maintained that New Englanders did not barbarize the English language, as the reviewer charged, by using it in peculiar ways. Americans who did so were not New Englanders. Further, while setting the women of Coventry against the backwoods rabble, he filled three pages with examples of barbarisms spoken by the lower classes of London: "duberous" for "dubious," "sinst" for "since," "sot" for "sat." Again his meaning was that he would not confuse English gentlemen with people who said "duberous," if English gentlemen would not confuse Jefferson with him.

The *koine,* the common speech, was particularly expressive to Dwight of the closeknit community centered in the white clapboard house. He assigned the widespread propriety in the use and pronunciation of English not only to New England's widespread literacy but also to its religious standards and its ingrained neighborliness. New Englanders go to church, where they hear correct pronunciation from the clergy. Friendly, educated New Englanders converse freely with their plain neighbors. While insisting on the correctness of New England speech, Dwight upheld, however, the usefulness of neologisms. He pointed out that the English themselves coin new words, and he added flatteringly that their language contains forty to seventy thousand words because it "is calculated for a people of great knowledge and many ideas to express."[6] Americans, he continued, coin such new words as the verb "progress" because they need them for new things. (According to Mencken's *American Language,* "progress" had flourished as an intransitive verb in England *ca.* 1590-1670, but had been dropped and reinvented in America. The first recorded use of "pioneer," incidentally, occurs in Dwight's *Travels.*)

Dwight did not wish Yankee English, however, to diverge far from the speech of educated London. He objected to the rapidity of Boston speech and to the "Boston style," "a phrase proverbially used throughout a considerable part of this country to denote a florid, pompous manner of writing."[7] Otherwise, he promised correct English readers that New Englanders spoke exactly like "well-bred people in London." The author of *Greenfield Hill* had risked naming wagons "wains" and bumpkins "Lawrences" for the sake of creating a native idiom. The prodigal son sought a language in which friendly overtures would not offend the ears of civil Englishmen.

Dwight's specifically literary views had also changed. At nineteen "our American poet" had transformed the Yale curriculum to take literature away from politics and had delivered a commencement address boldly treating the Bible as poetry. But by 1812 his esthetic criteria had become wholly moralistic and political. He now taught rhetoric to his class from Hugh Blair, whose standards were at once esthetic and moral. National culture he now identified with national morals: "Sound taste, sound sense, and sound morals go together: this is the law of the universe." His survey of human history convinced him that the periods of "good national taste" were always those of national rectitude. What good English writers had been bad men, were "the best among the bad." Looking back on the period of his youth he denounced its tastes, as he denounced its hopes, as corrupt; and he blamed the skeptical Gibbon for corrupting them. According to Dwight's "law of the universe," taste rose during the religious revivals (when he, paradoxically, stopped writing poetry). The rule-breaking epic poet proclaimed that "nature ought to be consulted in preference to Aristotle."[8] The traditionalist told the members of the senior class that, before fixing their own standards, they must "recover all the standards of the ancients: we cannot make a new one."

Having reduced literature to morals, Dwight no longer felt that one kind of government fostered the arts more than another. Earlier he had equated Independence with a new spirit of inquiry which would create unprecedented achievements in music, painting, and poetry. Now he acknowledged glumly that republican America had shown itself unwilling to patronize culture: "No American has, within my knowledge, been willing to inhabit a garret for the sake of becoming an author." But he wished Englishmen to acknowledge that monarchical England, where Milton and Dryden had died beggars, had been far from encouraging its writers and had acted toward them capriciously. On his moralistic basis he even granted American literature a narrow superiority:

while no obscene book had been published in America, most English plays and novels, and many English songs and poems "have been scandalously obscene and polluted."

In some specific instances, too, Dwight thought, American literature surpassed English. He preferred John Marshall's life of Washington to any English biography except Johnson's *Lives of the English Poets,* and some American oratory to most English. Of course his main example of American genius was Jonathan Edwards, whose metaphysical power he considered unequaled. In the *Travels* his six pages of praise to his grandfather were climaxed by the opinion that the loss of Edwards' works would be more grievous to mankind than the loss of the "whole works of half the ancient writers now extant." As further evidence of American culture he adduced, with brief mention, Benjamin Franklin, David Rittenhouse, John Singleton Copley, Benjamin West, Gilbert Stuart, Cotton Mather, and, generously, Ezra Stiles. He defended John Trumbull, once his fellow tutor, against British detractors as being little inferior in wit to Samuel Butler, and in other ways superior. Cordially, Dwight granted that Trumbull lampooned England, and cordially added that Butler lampooned Presbyterians. As a token of his good wishes, he admitted to laughing at *Hudibras* and urged fraternally minded Englishmen to enjoy *M'Fingal.*

Dwight explained the failure of America to bring forth the new Popes and new Addisons he had prophesied by citing a lack of financial "motives" and by three other obstacles. Sharing a common language with England, Americans could use English books and had no need to produce their own. Also, the clergy, of New England at least, gave their time to the salvation of their flocks, not to ornamental but irrelevant accomplishments. Lastly, Americans concerned themselves rather with action than with thought. Still, Dwight felt that "as much has been done as in the circumstances could be reasonably expected." It was no small thing, he observed in the *Travels,* to convert forests into pleasant homes. In a comparable state of uncultivation, England had produced in the eighth century only Bede; in the ninth, only Alfred; in the tenth and eleventh, nothing. Whatever the accuracy of this explanation, it did not reflect Dwight's experience. In *The Conquest of Canäan,* he had argued the need for American books; and in *Greenfield Hill,* he had struggled against the language he shared with England. As a minister, he had concerned himself both with the salvation of his flock and with the writing of poems, and, as a man, both with action and thought.

What made Dwight an apologist for American culture was his own inability to appreciate it. Now nearly blind, he could seldom read longer than fifteen minutes a day. Even so, his moralistic and Federalistic criteria confined his reading to the Connecticut Wits and to the theologians of New England. Joel Barlow, the renegade Francophile, he politically and morally disowned, and offered up as a sacrifice to Anglo-Yankee friendship: "With Mr. *Barlow's Columbiad,* you have a right to take any decent liberty. He has treated your country in such a manner, as to be lawful game to a *Briton.* I shall, therefore, leave him in your hands." His modesty forcing him to omit himself as well, he thus thinned even the unimposing ranks of the Connecticut Wits. Philip Freneau his politics compelled him to damn as a "despicable tool of bigger incendiaries."[9] Noah Webster he dismissed for personal reasons, dating back to Webster's harsh review of *The Triumph of Infidelity.* William Dunlap, his own brother-in-law, he omitted because he hated plays.

Apart from Shakespeare's tragedies, Dwight believed that plays did not instruct, gave imperfect pictures of human nature, and aroused immoral tendencies by allowing men to appear in women's clothes, by letting loose emotions before a crowd, and by according admiration to actors and actresses, "beings as polluted as it is possible for the mind to conceive." The money spent on the New York theater alone, he scowled, would support all the ministers in any county of Connecticut. He decided that the only comedy which a "Christian could read without pain" was General Burgoyne's *The Heiress.*

For many reasons Dwight was no longer able to appreciate his times. His temperament weakened his defense of American culture by forcing him to exclude the considerable recent flourishing of poems, novels, and plays by American writers. For his defense he might have cited Joel Barlow, Philip Freneau, William Dunlap, Thomas Godfrey, Nathaniel Evans, Francis Hopkinson, Royall Tyler, Charles Brockden Brown, Hugh Henry Brackenridge, James Kirke Paulding, and Washington Irving. But he prized none of them. He could not admit them into his *Remarks;* for, by suggesting that America had begun to achieve its cultural independence, they made his hope of Anglo-Yankee partnership seem unnecessary and untimely. They made him seem a voice of the past.

III *The New Era*

Now came the ending of Connecticut Federalism itself.

In February, 1816, Republican-Episcopalian citizens from all over Connecticut convened in New Haven to establish an opposition party presenting a united front against political Congregationalism. For governor they nominated Oliver Wolcott, on a platform of ecclesiastical reform aimed at breaking the religious establishment for all time. The appeal of this "American ticket" in the sectarian towns was great. For the first time, Hartford failed to return Federalists to the legislature. With Wolcott's election in 1817 the regime of the Puritan governors of Connecticut ended. A year later the state had a new constitution which ultimately abolished tithes, eliminated religious tests for public office, and cut the quasi-legal bond between Congregationalism and the state.[10]

The effect of this disestablishment on Dwight may be supposed. The other challenges to Congregational power had set in motion his millennial rhetoric, his tirades against infidels, and his anonymous proclamations of doomsday. But the disestablishment coincided with the ending of the war, and it occurred when Congregationalism in the state and religion throughout the country prospered. Genuinely revitalized, Congregationalism now thrived on the force of its own spiritual appeal; and Dwight detected a whole new unity in his religion. Nothing could threaten it, he felt, or must coerce it into being. He had seen the disestablishment coming, for he had treated it in his *Remarks* as an accomplished fact; the English establishment, he charged, produces sects and friction, while in New England the effect of disestablishment is "to make all men feel, that they possess the same religious rights; to induce them from this consideration to feel the same interest in the prosperity of the government which equally protects them all; and to live quietly and pleasantly by the side of each other."

These social feelings, this *pietas,* Dwight had attributed, in all his earlier writings, to precisely the opposite cause—to a state-supported church. It may be that in reversing his stand he was simply assenting to fate, defending the disestablishment as an irreversible, however sorry, fact. But he had always valued peace higher than virtue and had loved quiet more than causes. The peace of Connecticut guaranteed, he was satisfied.

Then, despite the disestablishment, the success of religion at home and of missionary work abroad led Dwight to declare that the era of revolution and turmoil that he had witnessed was past. In his last important work, a lengthy series of "Observations on the Present State of Religion in the World," he rejoiced that religion bloomed throughout America and Europe, that it had come back to the heart, that funds poured into the coffers of missionary societies, that congregations were fuller than at any time since the Revolution, that private religious assemblies multiplied, that religious tracts were widely read, that two hundred students entered into churches as a result of Yale revivals, that eighteen parish churches had sprung up on the road to New York, that not only were there more churches but more handsome and expensive ones, a fact which "always springs in some degree at least from piety."[11] He rejoiced, in short, over an era of good feelings and new beginnings.

The new health of religion roused the long inactive optimistic half of Dwight's manicheism. He greeted the era of disestablishment with the hopes and idealism of a second childhood. The world now seemed to him beautiful: "all the rude, gloomy, and gross scenes . . . have vanished. In their places have sprung up, as by the hand of a magician, landscapes only beautiful or sublime." In place of the wilderness and the long turbulence of the post-revolutionary era, he sighted "springs and rivers, the flowers and trees, the bloom, the beauty, and the immortality of Eden."[12]

The shrinking of Dwight's social focus, from transcontinental America to rural Connecticut, stopped. In the successes of the American Bible Society he saw new hope that all of America could be unified. A united Protestantism would diminish party spirit, which had long divided the country and stunted the growth of its arts and sciences. As at nineteen, he became the champion of Union, expecting "men of respectability in different parts of the Union to discern, and acknowledge each others' wisdom and worth."[13] Quite incredibly, he ended his "Observations" with the earliest idealistic vision of his youth—the dream of rising glory. His hopes sprang from revival Christianity, not from a secular theory of progress; but his tone and diction were precisely those of his first commencement address: "I am constrained to believe a new era in the moral concerns of man to have commenced; and anticipate from this period a new order of things, in the affairs of our world, in which Religion of the Gospel will rise in all its majesty, beneficence, and glory, to the astonished, and delighted view of mankind." Peace, love, and joy, he foresaw, would visit "every cottage, and what is more wonderful, every palace also; and spread from Greenland to *Cape Horn,* and from *Japan* to *California.*"[14]

Now sixty-four years old, Dwight resumed in this spirit not only the hopes of his youth but also its activities. He began writing verse and essays again. He published an irregular ode entitled "The Maniac of Gadara," his first poem in nearly twenty years. Here, as if to mark his rejuvenation, he retold the Gospel story in which Jesus miraculously restores an angry and unbalanced hermit to sweet sanity and manhood:

> Convuls'd, the fainting Maniac fell,
> And shriek'd to life his last farewell.
> Rais'd by MESSIAH'S hand, again he stood;
> With softer light his eyeballs glow'd;
> His cheeks the crimson flush'd anew;
> And glistering dropp'd the grateful dew.
> Arrayed in man's attire, with aspect mild
> He knew himself a man, and spoke, and smil'd.[15]

Dwight also completed six new numbers of "The Friend" for a magazine he hoped to establish. He wrote a fifteen hundred line poem, "The Trial," in which genius and common sense contest, with truth as umpire. ("The Trial" and the essays have since become lost.) He composed and preached a series of sermons, enough for a whole volume, on the evidences of divine revelation.

But in 1816, amidst this remarkable revival of his youthful aspirations and ideals, Dwight's health collapsed. For a year he carried on in excruciating pain with cancer of the bladder, and died on January 11, 1817. His death, Jedediah Morse lamented, would be felt more keenly than the death of any other man in America.[16] Lyman Beecher burst into tears in his pulpit and cried "My Father! my father!"[17] New Haven suspended business. Throughout the country, services and sermons marked Dwight's passing.

Dwight's works have not survived as well as his name. He did not think profoundly on the issues of his age, or explain them in memorable prose, or in verse of any quality. He is seen most flatteringly in his life. What he said counted less than where he said it—the pulpit of Jonathan Edwards or the Yale presidency—and less than what his listeners believed he represented. For he incarnated and kept alive, as no one else in his time, the character of seventeenth-century New England.

On one side, Dwight shared the most advanced sentiments of the Enlightenment: its delight in reason, its hopes for penal reform and an end to slavery, its fascination with such signs of progress as bridges and canals. But, on the other side, he embodied the sense of human weakness, limitation, and doom of 1630. He endorsed the theory of progress, and he saw America advancing to some form of perfection; but lividly he also saw perpetually sinning man as hellbent toward the flames of God's wrath. He foresaw a splendiferous imperial America, and also a Puritan America of small city-states where men, as William Penn said, become happy by living near to one another and conversing often with one another.

Drastically, Dwight shifted from one side to the other as events dictated: in 1775 he rejoiced that Americans "have learned to despise the shackles of custom"; in 1781 he despaired over their "universal levity and corruption"; by 1800 he rejoiced again that "the Christian world has already roused itself from the slumber of two centuries"; by 1812 he despaired again that "at no time, since the deluge, has the situation of the human race been so extraordinary, the world so shaken"; by 1816 he once more rejoiced over "a new era in the moral concerns of man."

Dwight was in this sense a manichean: he lived only on birthday or doomsday. He understood only the Conquest of Canaan or the Triumph of Infidelity. His mind never grew. For each occasion he owned a separate voice: for doomsday, the language of the Puritan Jeremiads; for birthday, the couplets and balanced sentences of neo-Classic verse and prose. He brought out one or the other as circumstances required, but he never fully bent his style to discovering new circumstances. His divided temperament doomed his poetry to jumping from Joshua to "a Mr. Mercer," from Columbia to the Connecticut Valley, from "temples starr'd with gems" to log cabins, from visions to revisions.

These disconnections record not only Dwight's conflicts or his lack of talent, however; they characterize much of the native verse of his time, which celebrates a nation of vast promise and limited achievements. With that nation's faltering growth Dwight was, finally, impatient. Men in different parts of the Union were not likely to become completely alien to one another, or completely to acknowledge one another's worth. The nation would neither be wholly unlike Connecticut, nor completely like it. But Dwight would compromise little and sacrifice nothing; and he would not wait. Until the last year of his life, he stopped writing poetry and celebrating America. "Our American poet" became the statistician of the continuity of New England ways.

The best eulogy on Dwight, for it suggested the kinship between the divided man and the place he lived in, came from Samuel Goodrich, later the author of nationalistic children's books. A character with such "lights and shades," he said, could be produced only in the "stern but kindly" climate of New England, "our cold northern Nazareth."[18] In Europe one may find men of genius but not, by contrast, men of such large common sense and high moral principles, "hardly of the Puritan type, so well illustrated in the life and character of Timothy Dwight."

Notes and References

N.B. To avoid excessive annotation I have supplied only an initial note for Dwight's shorter works. Subsequent quotations from those works can easily be found without benefit of page numbers. For substantial quotations from Dwight's longer works, however, I have supplied page references in the text.

Chapter One

1. Quoted in Leon Howard, *The Connecticut Wits* (Chicago, 1943), p. 834.
2. Benjamin Silliman, *A Sketch of the Life and Character of President Dwight* (New Haven, 1817), p. 6.
3. Howard, pp. 83-4.
4. Franklin B. Dexter (ed.), *The Literary Diary of Ezra Stiles* (New York, 1901), II, 531.
5. On the popularity of these views see Merrill Jensen, *The New Nation: A History of the United States During the Confederation 1781-1789* (New York, 1958), chap. 4, "The Spirit of the New Nation."
6. *America: or, a Poem on the Settlement of the British Colonies* (New Haven, n.d.), p. 9.
7. Jared Sparks (ed.), *Correspondence of the American Revolution* (Boston, 1853), II, 81-2.
8. John C. Fitzpatrick (ed.), *The Writings of George Washington from the Original Manuscript Sources 1745-1799* (Washington, 1834), XI, 105-6.
9. Theodore A. Zunder, *The Early Days of Joel Barlow* (New Haven, 1934), p. 165.
10. George Sensabaugh, *Milton in Early America* (Princeton, 1964), chap. 4, "The Early Republic."
11. *A Dissertation on the History, Eloquence, and Poetry of the Bible* (New Haven, 1772), p. 11.
12. See Vincent Freimarck, "Timothy Dwight's *Dissertation on the Bible*," *American Literature*, XXIV (March, 1952), 73-77 and Donald M. Foerster, *The Fortunes of Epic Poetry: A Study in English and American Criticism 1750-1950* (The Catholic University of America Press, n. pl., 1962), chap. 1, "Homage and Doubt in the Neo-classical Period."
13. Henry Adams, *The United States in 1800* (1889; repr. Ithaca, 1960), p. 68.
14. Theodore A. Zunder, "Noah Webster and *The Conquest of Canaan*," *American Literature*, I (May, 1929), 200-202.
15. *Ibid.*
16. Miltonic parallels were equally popular. Many poets used *Paradise Lost* to justify or deride the Revolution. The poem's struggle between good and evil, its sense of a great subject, its treatment of Adam all provided suggestive parallels. The Tory satirist Jonathan Odell, for instance, wrote:

> What Michael to the first arch-rebel said,
> Well would rebuke the rebel army's head;
> What Satan to th'angelic Prince replied,
> Such are the words of Continental pride . . .
>
> (*The American Times*, London, 1780)

In effect, *Paradise Lost* produced in America a set of ideological conventions. Later, Milton was frequently used, as Dwight used him, in answer to Deists, infidels, and skeptics. Federalists attached to Jacobin clubs the image of the infernal council, and used Milton's description of Hell to describe France. See Sensabaugh, *op. cit.*, chap. 3.

17. *A Sermon, preached at Stamford . . . upon the General Thanksgiving, Dec. 18th, 1777* (Hartford, 1778), p. 9.

18. *A Discourse . . . on the Character of George Washington, Esq.* (New Haven, 1800), p. 17.

19. *A Valedictory Address to the Young Gentlemen . . . at Yale-College, July 25th, 1776* (New Haven, 1776), p. 12.

20. "Columbia: a Song," *American Museum,* III (June, 1787), 484.

21. William Cowper, *Works,* ed. Robert Southey (London, 1836), p. 316. Southey himself, who borrowed a copy from Humphreys, thought the work had "certainly some merit" in it.

22. William B. Cairns, *British Criticism of American Writing 1783-1815, University of Wisconsin Studies,* I (Madison, 1918), 65.

23. [Noah Webster], "To the Author of the Conquest of Canaan," *American Magazine,* March, 1788, p. 266.

24. *American Mercury,* September 1, 1788, in reply to "Miscellaneous Thoughts on the Poems of Mess'rs. Dwight and Barlow," in the preceding issue.

25. Joel Barlow, *The Vision of Columbus* (Hartford, 1787), p. 212.

26. Joseph Dennie, *Farmer's Museum or Lay Preacher's Gazette,* April 8, 1799, p. 1.

27. "The Critics. A Fable," *Gazette of the United States,* July 13, 1791, p. 2.

28. "The Friend. No. 4," *American Museum,* V (June, 1789), 566.

29. Roy Harvey Pearce, *The Continuity of American Poetry* (Princeton, 1961), p. 61.

30. *Ibid.,* p. 133.

Chapter Two

1. "Epistle from Dr. Dwight to Col. Humphreys," *The Miscellaneous Works of Colonel Humphreys* (New York, 1790), p. 107.

2. "The Friend. No. 3," *American Museum,* V (May, 1789), 445.

3. "The Friend. No. 5," *American Museum,* VI (August, 1789), 54.

4. "an essay on the judgment of history concerning America [*sic*]," *New Haven Gazette and the Connecticut Magazine,* II (April, 1787), 60.

5. "Address of the genius of Columbia to the members of the continental convention [*sic*]," *American Museum,* I (June, 1787), 483.

6. *Greenfield Hill: A Poem, in Seven Parts* (New York, 1794), p. 5.

7. William Penn, quoted in Dwight's "Observations on the Present State of Religion in the World," *Religious Intelligencer,* I (September 14, 1816), 242.

8. "Observations on Language," *Memoirs of the Connecticut Academy of Arts and Sciences,* I (New Haven, 1810), 365.

9. Quoted in Howard, *Wits,* p. 322.

10. Unfortunately, the details of Stiles's feud with Dwight are unknown. The relevant parts of Stiles's diary were destroyed after his death. See Edmund S. Morgan, *The Gentle Puritan: A Life of Ezra Stiles 1727-1795* (New Haven, 1962), pp. 344ff. One staff member of Dwight's Northampton school was Joel

Barlow, who with Dwight's encouragement completed while there a prose draft of the entire "Vision of Columbus."

11. John Adams was also troubled by the problem. In 1819 he asked Thomas Jefferson to "tell me how to prevent riches from becoming the effects of temperance and industry? Will you tell me how to prevent riches from producing luxury? Will you tell me how to prevent luxury from producing effeminacy, intoxication extravagance Vice and folly?" Lester J. Cappon (ed.), *The Adams-Jefferson Letters* (Chapel Hill, 1959), II, 551.

Chapter Three

1. *A Sermon, Preached at Northampton. . . occasioned by the Capture of the British Army. . .* (Hartford, [1781?]), p. 32.

2. On the causes of the rise of freethought in America, see G. Adolf Koch, *Republican Religion: The American Revolution and the Cult of Reason* (New York, 1933). Stiles's remark appears on p. 239.

3. The evidence of Dwight's authorship, if the reader will pardon a rather mechanical demonstration, is persuasive:

Greenfield Hill	*Triumph of Infidelity*
First guilt, first woe, first infamy of man,/Thou spot of hell, deep smirch'd on human kind,/The uncur'd gangrene of the reasoning mind.	This vast machine, so wondrous, so refin'd,/First, fairest offspring even of Satan's mind.
O slavery! laurel of the Infernal mind,/Proud Satan's triumph over lost mankind.	Blush, Satan, blush, thou sovereign of mankind,/When, what thy reptile foes, thou call'st to mind.
Nice Monboddo calculate their tails.	Mankind, when they wore tails, as Lord monboddo has most ingeniously proved.
this bad earth	this bad world
sooty car [slavery's]	sooty flight [Satan's]

Further parallels may be drawn between the *Triumph* and Dwight's later poem, "The Retrospect" (see the end of this chapter). "The Retrospect" raises the same charges against the French Revolutionists that the *Triumph* does against French Infidels. Both poems have the same meter and diction; both employ the device of panning from country to country in order to depict the spread of false ideas; both elaborate the theme of "False friends"; both treat the victims of Fashion as "dogs." Satan's flight in the *Triumph* duplicates the flight of the "form" in "The Retrospect": Satan goes a "sooty flight" in a "sooty car," the "form" moves on "sooty wings"; both have "pinions," both are preceded by a "clarion," both are compared to "dragons," both are "borne on clouds." The two poems use the same rhymes. Indeed, in the *Triumph* Dwight repeatedly ends on his favorite rhymes of "rise-skies" and "train-plain." In the *Triumph* "rise-skies" appears seven times exactly, and eight more with slight variants.

The *Triumph* parallels Dwight's other works as well. *Triumph*: "Man, that illustrious brute of noblest shape,/A swine unbristled, and an untailed ape." Compare the "Epistle to Col. Humphreys": "Of all the plagues that rise in human shape,/Good Heaven, preserve us from the travell'd Ape." Also, see Lewis Leary, "The Author of *The Triumph of Infidelity*," *New England Quarterly*, XX (September, 1947), 377-85.

4. *The Triumph of Infidelity: A Poem* ("Printed in the World," 1788), p. 5.

5. One suggested reading of the final line is that Satan's victory is a push-over since the enemy has all along been on Satan's side. There is no "friend of virtue"; all men are sinful. In the B text of the poem, published the same year, the line appeared "And to his cause NO FRIEND OF VIRTUE won." For this view, and a comparison of the two texts, see Jack Stillinger, "Dwight's *Triumph of Infidelity*: Text and Interpretation," *Studies in Bibliography*, XV (1962), 259-66.

6. "Address to the Ministers of the Gospel of every Denomination in the United States," *American Museum*, IV (July, 1788), 34.

7. The attack on Chauncy for glossing the page "with pains" is interesting, since Dwight himself could read very little without paining his eyes. The poem often refers to failing sight, making Dwight's authorship even more likely: "Now palsied age has dimm'd his mental sight"; Milton was "stone blind in his bodily eyes, but had clear and intuitive moral optics." Later Dwight describes Hume as Satan's "Amanuensis." Dwight regularly used an amanuensis himself because of his weak eyes. Ezra Stiles claimed, however, that Dwight only affected his myopia.

8. Noah Webster, "Review of New Publications," *American Magazine*, July, 1788, p. 590.

9. Dexter, *Diary of Stiles*, III, 326.

10. Quoted in Cairns, *British Criticisms*, 67-68.

11. *Virtuous Rulers a National Blessing* (Hartford, 1791), p. 18.

12. *The True Means of Establishing Public Happiness* (New Haven, 1795), p. 36.

13. *Sermons* (New Haven, 1828), I, 303-304.

14. *The Nature, and Danger, of Infidel Philosophy* (New Haven, 1798), p. 38.

15. *Ibid.*, p. 19.

16. *The Duty of Americans, at the Present Crisis* (New Haven, 1798), p. 11.

17. Quoted in Charles E. Cuningham, *Timothy Dwight 1752-1817* (New York, 1942), p. 342.

18. *Ibid.*

19. Anonymous review, *American Mercury*, February 24, 1803.

20. "Triumph of Infidelity Resuscitated," *American Mercury*, January 27, 1803. John Adams remembered that Hamilton had journeyed to Boston and Providence to persuade some people to throw away their votes, so that Adams would not have the unanimous support of New England. Thus Pinckney might be brought in as President; Adams, as Vice-President. Among those to whom Hamilton suggested this were "the learned and pious Doctors Dwight and Babcock." Dwight, Adams said, repeatedly urged, "we must sacrifice Adams, we must sacrifice Adams" (to whom, incidentally, Dwight had dedicated *Greenfield Hill*). C.F.A. Adams (ed.), *The Life and Works of John Adams* (Boston, 1850-1856), X, 124-25.

21. "Address to the Ministers," p. 33.
22. See Leary, "The Author of *The Triumph of Infidelity.*"
23. Quoted in Robert Edson Lee, "Timothy Dwight and the Boston *Palladium,*" *New England Quarterly,* XXXV (June, 1962), 232.
24. *Ibid.,* p. 233.
25. "To the Farmers and Mechanics of New-England," *New-England Palladium,* XVII (May 26, 1801).
26. "Farmer Johnson's Political Catechism," *Mercury and New-England Palladium,* XVII (April 14, 1801).
27. "Morpheus," *Mercury and New-England Palladium,* XVIII (November 27, 1801).
28. *Ibid.,* December 11, 1801.
29. *Ibid.,* December 15, 1801.
30. "Rights of Women," *Mercury and New-England Palladium,* XIX (March 2, 1802).
31. *Diary of William Dunlap* (New York, 1931), I, 207.
32. "An Extract from 'The Retrospect,'" *Mercury and New-England Palladium,* XVII (January 2, 1801). In a letter to the editor Dwight told of writing the poem in 1796 and of adding to it in 1797. He expressed his hope that the subject was not outdated.

Chapter Four

1. Quoted in Cuningham, *Timothy Dwight,* p. 304.
2. See Edmund S. Morgan, "Ezra Stiles and Timothy Dwight," *Proceedings of the Massachusetts Historical Society,* LXXII (Boston, 1963), 101-17.
3. *A Sermon Preached at the Opening of the Theological Institution in Andover* (Boston, 1808), p. 14.
4. On these changes in the character of Connecticut Congregationalism during the revivals, see Charles Roy Keller, *The Second Great Awakening in Connecticut* (New Haven, 1942).
5. *The Charitable Blessed* (New Haven, 1810), p. 21.
6. On the entry of humanitarian views into Calvinism, see Joseph Haroutunian, *Piety Versus Moralism: The Passing of the New England Theology* (New York, 1932). This emphasis on social benevolence and good works did not, however, transform Dwight's essential conservatism. Many of the well-to-do found it desirable to sponsor charitable agencies, which by soothing the poor and the disenfranchised nipped radicalism in the bud. See Clifford S. Griffin, "Religious Benevolence as Social Control, 1815-1860," *Mississippi Valley Historical Review,* XLIV (December, 1957), 423-44.
7. Moses Coit Tyler, *Three Men of Letters* (New York, 1895), p. 124.
8. *Travels; in New-England and New York* (New Haven, 1821-22), I, 165.
9. Facsimile letter in Cuningham, facing p. 344.
10. See Gilbert Chinard, "Eighteenth Century Theories on America as a Human Habitat," *Proceedings of the American Philosophical Society,* XCI (1947), 27-57.
11. Occasionally, dissenting children were freed from attendance. See Richard J. Purcell, *Connecticut in Transition: 1775-1818* (1918; repr. Middletown, Conn., 1963), pp. 63-64.

12. Dwight pointed out that New Yorkers, too, can carry arms, and he admired New York for having the best police of any American city. He retracted both compliments by adding that New York needs arms and police because of its explosive mixture of races and nationalities.

13. Purcell, p. 98.

14. Robert Southey, reviewing the *Travels* anonymously in the *Quarterly Review* in 1823, pointed out a contradiction in Dwight's thinking on this point. On the one hand, Dwight says that America is not savage; on the other, that the West drains off the savage element. The reason life in Connecticut is so mild, Southey speculated, is not that its institutions are perfect but that its malcontents move to the frontier.

15. *An Address, to the Emigrants from Connecticut* (Hartford, 1817), p. 5.

Chapter Five

1. *A Discourse . . . on the Public Fast* (New Haven, 1812), p. 6.

2. Letter to Oliver Wolcott, in George Gibbs (ed.), *Memoirs of the Administrations of Washington and John Adams* (New York, 1846), I, 107.

3. This "Decision" was transcribed from a student notebook, and delivered in answer to John Caldwell Calhoun, then a Yale junior and ardent Jeffersonian. See Abe C. Ravitz, "Timothy Dwight's Decisions," *New England Quarterly,* XXXI (December, 1958), 516-17.

4. Theodore Dwight (ed.), *President Dwight's Decisions of Questions Discussed by the Senior Class in Yale College in 1813 and 1814* (New York, 1833), p. 335.

5. *Remarks on the Review of Inchiquin's Letters* (Boston, 1815), p. 14.

6. Quoted in Abe C. Ravitz, "Timothy Dwight: Professor of Rhetoric," *New England Quarterly,* XXIX (March, 1956), 67. Dwight added that the Indian language has only two to three thousand words.

7. Dwight also disliked the Boston addiction to fashionable education for women. He explained the gloominess of Boston girls by their reading of novels and plays, which made them dreamy and utopian, and disappointed with the real world. Like T. S. Eliot, who found Boston and Cambridge refined beyond the point of civilization, Dwight felt that its "taste for living has become too refined, too dainty, to relish anything in real life" (*Travels,* I, 476).

8. "The friend. No. 4 [*sic*]," *American Museum,* V (June, 1789), 567.

9. Letter to Wolcott.

10. Purcell, *op. cit.,* suggests that the Federalists were defeated largely because the Congregationalist clergy did not participate to any extent in the election, and had ceased preaching anti-Republicanism. Perhaps, he speculates, they decided not to campaign after the Hartford convention of 1814, which discredited them (at the time Dwight himself lamented that politics had engulfed religion); perhaps their attention was engrossed by the revivals; perhaps they realized the justice of accusations against their politicking; perhaps the awakening itself developed the principle of voluntary support of religion; perhaps the Republicans had proven that they were not diabolic Infidels set upon destroying public order. For whatever reasons, the connection between church and state was broken.

11. "Observations on the Present State of Religion in the World," *Religious Intelligencer,* I (August 17, 1816), 178.

12. *Ibid.*, September 7, 1816, p. 228.
13. *Ibid.*, September 14, 1816, p. 244.
14. *Ibid.*, pp. 245-46.
15. "The Maniac of Gadara, An Irregular Ode," *Panoplist*, November, 1816, p. 528. The Gospel account appears in Matt. 8:28, Mark 5:21, Luke 8:26.
16. Quoted in Cuningham, p. 352.
17. Lyman Beecher, *Autobiography, Correspondence, etc.* (New York, 1871), I, 331.
18. S. G. Goodrich, *Recollections of a Lifetime* (New York, 1857), I, 347-48.

Selected Bibliography

Dwight's writings are fairly well covered in Jacob Blanck, *Bibliography of American Literature,* II (New Haven, 1957). Blanck omits, however, many of Dwight's anonymous publications. Supplementary bibliographies appear in Cuningham and Howard, below. Further "Decisions" by Dwight are reprinted in Abe C. Ravitz, "Timothy Dwight: Professor of Rhetoric," *New England Quarterly,* XXIX (March, 1956), 63-72 and in the same author's "Timothy Dwight's Decisions," *New England Quarterly,* XXXI (December, 1958), 514-19. For other possible contributions by Dwight to the *Palladium,* see Lee, below. There are no large collections of Dwight manuscripts. Most of his papers were lost, or scattered among his descendants. A list of extant manuscripts appears in Cuningham.

PRIMARY SOURCES

Dwight's works were, in whole and part, widely reprinted in his lifetime. A full list of reprints appears in Blanck. The following selective list includes only the first printings of his works, with the exception of the *Friend* essays, which originally appeared in the *New-Haven Gazette,* but are more accessible in the *American Museum.* The works are named chronologically according to publication dates:

Verse

America: or, a Poem on the Settlement of the British Colonies, New Haven (1780?).

"Columbia," *The Boston Magazine* (December, 1783), 71.

The Conquest of Canäan: A Poem, in Eleven Books. Hartford. Elisha Babcock, 1785.

"The Trial of Faith," *New-Haven Gazette, and the Connecticut Magazine,* September 21, October 12 and 19, 1786, pp. 245-46, 269-70, 277-78.

"Address of the genius of Columbia to the members of the continental convention," *American Museum,* I (June, 1787), 482-84.

The Triumph of Infidelity: A Poem. "Printed in the World," 1788.

"The Seasons Moralized," *American Museum,* V (March, 1789), 302-303.

"A Song: written in 1771," *American Museum,* V (April, 1789), 408-09.

"A Hymn Sung at the Public Exhibition of the Scholars, Belonging to the Academy at Greenfield," *American Museum,* VI (August, 1789), 171-72.

"Epistle from Dr. Dwight to Col. Humphreys. Greenfield, 1785." *The Miscel-*

laneous Works of Colonel Humphreys. New York: Hodge, Allen, and Campbell, 1790. Pp. 102-10.

"The Critics. A Fable," *Gazette of the United States,* July 13, 1791, p. 2.

"Message of Mordecai to Esther," *American Poems, Selected and Original.* Litchfield: Collier and Buel, 1793. 299-304.

Greenfield Hill: A Poem, in Seven Parts. New York: Childs and Swaine, 1794.

"An Extract from 'The Retrospect,'" *New-England Palladium,* January 3, 1801.

"The Maniac of Gadara, An Irregular Ode," *Panoplist,* November, 1816, pp. 526-28.

Dwight's long poem, "The Trial," has apparently been lost. Manuscripts of his juvenile poem on Burgoyne's defeat and of his "poem on May, at 15 yrs. of Age" are in the Dartmouth college library. The most available selection of Dwight's verse is Vernon Louis Parrington's, *The Connecticut Wits* (New York, 1926). Parrington includes portions of the *Conquest* and *Greenfield Hill,* as well as the complete *Triumph,* "Columbia," "A Song," "A Hymn," "The Critics" and a psalm from Dwight's revision of Watts. The texts, however, were not prepared by Parrington himself, and are poorly edited.

Prose

A Dissertation on the History, Eloquence, and Poetry of the Bible. New Haven, 1772.

A Valedictory Address, New Haven, 1776.

A Sermon, preached at Stamford . . . upon the General Thanksgiving. Hartford, 1778.

A Sermon, Preached at Northampton . . . occasioned by the Capture of the British Army. Hartford (1781?)

"An essay on the judgment of history concerning America," *New-Haven Gazette and the Connecticut Magazine,* II (April 12, 1787), 59-60.

The Friend, Nos. 1-6, *American Museum,* V and VI (January 1789, March, May, June, August, and October 1789), 69-71, 220-22, 445-47, 564-67, 154-56, 283-86.

Virtuous Rulers a National Blessing. Hartford, 1791.

A Discourse, on the Genuineness and Authenticity of the New Testament. New York, 1794.

The True Means of Establishing Public Happiness. New Haven, 1795.

The Nature, and Danger, of Infidel Philosophy. New Haven, 1798.

The Duty of Americans, at the Present Crisis. New Haven, 1798.

"To the Farmers and Mechanics of New-England," *New-England Palladium,* May 12-June 5, 1801.

"Farmer Johnson's Political Catechism," *Mercury and New-England Palladium,* March 31, April 3, 14, 17, May 8, 1801.

"Morpheus," *Mercury and New-England Palladium,* November 24, 27, December 8, 11, 15, 1801 and March 2, 5, 9, 1802.

"Observations on Language," *Memoirs of the Connecticut Academy of Arts and Sciences.* New Haven, 1810, I, 365-86.

A Discourse . . . on the Public Fast. New Haven, 1812.

"Lectures on the Evidences of Divine Revelation," *Panoplist, and Missionary*

Magazine United, June-December 1810, January-March and June-September 1811, January, March, May 1812, June-August 1813.

Remarks on the Review of Inchiquin's Letters. Boston: Samuel T. Armstrong, 1815.

"Observations on the Present State of Religion in the World," *Religious Intelligencer,* August 10, 17, 24, 31, September 7, 14, 1816.

An Address, to the Emigrants from Connecticut. Hartford, 1817.

Theology; explained and defended. 5 vols. Middletown, Conn.: Clark and Lyman, 1818-19.

Travels; In New-England and New York. 4 vols. New Haven: S. Converse, 1821-22.

Decisions of Questions Discussed by the Senior Class . . . in 1813 and 1814, ed. Theodore Dwight. New York: Jonathan Leavitt, 1833.

SECONDARY SOURCES

ALDRIDGE, ALFRED OWEN. "Timothy Dwight's Posthumous Gift to British Theology," *American Literature,* XXI (January, 1950), 479-81. Influence of Dwight's *Theology* on one of England's most famous biblical scholars, Thomas Hartwell Horne, who lifted verbatim Dwight's analytic outline of Deistic philosophy.

BEECHER, LYMAN. *Autobiography.* Cambridge: Harvard University Press, 1961. Credits Dwight with the revivals at Yale, a view challenged in Morgan, below.

BUCHANAN, LEWIS E. "The Ethical Ideas of Timothy Dwight," *Research Studies of the State College of Washington,* XIII (September, 1945). Lucid account, in general terms, of Dwight's moral philosophy as revealed in the five volumes of his *Theology.*

CAIRNS, WILLIAM B. *British Criticisms of American Writings 1783-1815. University of Wisconsin Studies,* I. Madison: The University, 1918. Reprints and discusses British reviews of Dwight's writings.

CUNINGHAM, CHARLES E. *Timothy Dwight 1752-1817: A Biography.* New York: The Macmillan Company, 1942. Treats Dwight primarily as an educator, with lengthy paraphrases of his prose works. Hardly mentions his verse.

FREIMARCK, VINCENT. "Timothy Dwight's *Dissertation on the Bible," American Literature,* XXIV (March, 1952), 73-77. Shows that most of Dwight's arguments derived from the Yale library, despite his professed originality.

———. "Rhetoric at Yale in 1807," *Proceedings of the American Philosophical Society,* CX (August, 1966), 235-55. Reprints a splendidly detailed notebook kept by a student in Dwight's rhetoric class.

GABRIEL, RALPH HENRY. *Religion and Learning at Yale.* New Haven: Yale University Press, 1958, Chap. 4, "Timothy Dwight." Fresh appraisal of Dwight's presidency; places him in the tradition of the Reformation as a champion of science and religion. Stresses how Dwight spurred on the revitalization of Protestantism in America after the Revolution, with much new information on his part in the revivals.

GOODRICH, S. G. *Recollections of a Lifetime.* New York: Auburn, Miller, Orton and Mulligan, 1857. Important biographical information on Dwight, furnished by his nephew Theodore.

GRISWOLD, A. WHITNEY. "Three Puritans on Prosperity," *New England Quarterly*, VII (September, 1934), 475-93. Compares Dwight with Mather and Franklin as disciples of the Protestant Ethic.

HAROUTUNIAN, JOSEPH. *Piety Versus Moralism: The Passing of the New England Theology*. New York: Henry Holt and Company, 1932. Describes how Dwight adopted humanitarian views into his Calvinism.

HOWARD, LEON. *The Connecticut Wits*. Chicago: University of Chicago Press, 1943. Excellent on the development of Dwight's ideas and on placing Dwight among the other Wits. Takes Dwight's rhetoric a bit literally, however, without accounting for the political realities behind it.

KELLER, CHARLES ROY. *The Second Great Awakening in Connecticut*. New Haven: Yale University Press, 1942. Treats Dwight as the head of the New Divinity clergy. Analyzes his strictly religious appeal, apart from his politics, an antidote to Purcell, below.

KOCH, G. ADOLF. *Republican Religion*. New York: Henry Holt and Company, 1933. Traces the rise of Infidelity in the colonies, Dwight's opposition to it, and counterattacks against Dwight.

LEARY, LEWIS. "The Author of *The Triumph of Infidelity*," *New England Quarterly*, XX (September, 1947), 377-85. An important discussion of the poem, pointing out parallels in Dwight's other works and identifying the pseudonymous characters.

LEE, ROBERT EDSON. "Timothy Dwight and the Boston *Palladium*," *New England Quarterly*, XXXV (June, 1962), 229-39. Account of the Federalist-Congregationalist attempt to establish and distribute their own journal of opinion. Identifies and discusses Dwight's contributions.

MORGAN, EDMUND S. "Ezra Stiles and Timothy Dwight," *Proceedings of the Massachusetts Historical Society*, LXXII (Boston, 1963), 101-17. An important challenge to the view that Dwight rescued Yale and America from Infidelity. A shrewd appraisal of Dwight's part in the revivals in full view of the available facts. Still, little is known of the actual relation between Stiles and Dwight. Further material appears in the author's *The Gentle Puritan: A Life of Ezra Stiles 1727-1795*. New Haven: Yale University Press, 1962.

PARRINGTON, VERNON LOUIS. *The Connecticut Wits*. New York: Harcourt, Brace & Company, 1926. Condescending treatment of Dwight as "a walking repository of the venerable status quo." Sees Dwight's reputation as undeservedly inflated by contemporaries. Largely reprinted in the author's *The Colonial Mind*. New York: Harcourt, Brace & Company, 1927.

PURCELL, RICHARD J. *Connecticut in Transition: 1775-1818*. 1918, repr. Middletown: Wesleyan University Press, 1963. Very important background material for Dwight's writings. Details Dwight's part in the change of Connecticut from a church-and-state oligarchy to a democracy. Suggests that the charges of indiscreet political activity leveled against Dwight were exaggerated.

RICHARDSON, LYON. *Early American Magazines 1741-1789*. New York: Columbia University Press, 1931. Material on the relations between Dwight, Webster, and Matthew Carey. Identifies several anonymous pieces by Dwight.

SENSABAUGH, GEORGE. *Milton in Early America.* New Jersey: Princeton University Press, 1964. Milton's influence on *The Conquest of Canäan,* particularly elements of Satan's character in Joshua.

SILLIMAN, BENJAMIN. *A Sketch of the Life and Character of President Dwight.* New Haven: Maltby, Goldsmith & Co., 1817. Mainly eulogistic. Depicts Dwight's cordiality and versatility in governing the college.

SPRAGUE, WILLIAM B. "Life of Timothy Dwight." In JARED SPARKS (ed.). *The Library of American Biography.* Boston: Charles C. Little and James Brown, 1845. IV, 225-364. Mainly hagiography, but an important source of biographical material.

———. "Memoir of the Life of President Dwight." In Dwight's *Theology.* London: Thomas Tegg, 1831. I, v-lxxi. The chief source of biographical material on Dwight, on which all later biographers rely.

STILLINGER, JACK. "Dwight's *Triumph of Infidelity*: Text and Interpretation," *Studies in Bibliography,* XV (1962), 259-66. Compares the "A" and "B" texts of the poem, published in the same year.

TYLER, MOSES COIT. *Three Men of Letters.* New York: H. P. Putnam's Sons, 1895. Chap. 2, "A Great College President and What he Wrote." A patronizing discussion of "our hero." Very harsh on Dwight's writings, which Tyler finds monotonous, redundant, and commonplace.

ZUNDER, THEODORE A. "Noah Webster and *The Conquest of Canaan,*" *American Literature,* I (May, 1929), 200-202. Reprints Dwight's letter to Webster detailing the history of the poem's composition and commenting on the allegorical interpretation.

Index

Index

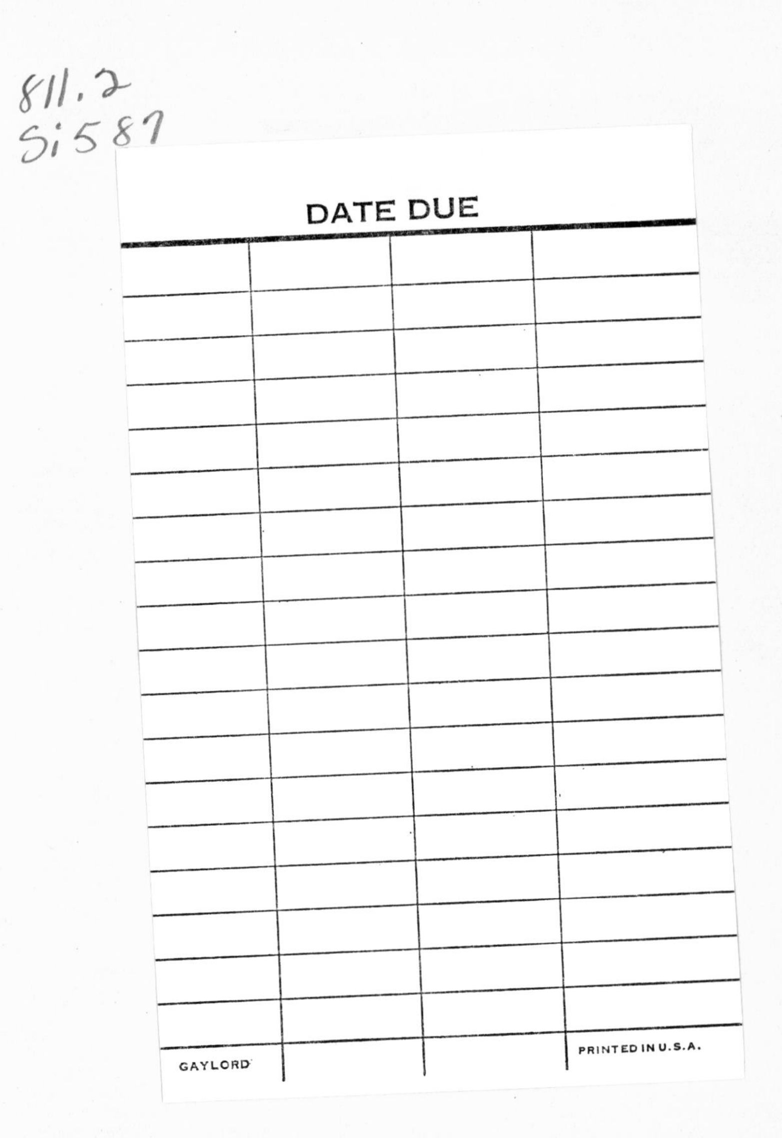
DATE DUE
GAYLORD
PRINTED IN U.S.A.